UNFOLDED

INDIA'S AIR DEFENCE FROM WWII TO OPERATION SINDOOR

Also by the Author

The POW Who Saved Kashmir—
Unsung Saga of Sher Bacha Brig Pritam Singh, MC

UNFOLDED
INDIA'S AIR DEFENCE FROM WWII TO OPERATION SINDOOR

Pankaj P Singh

Title: Unfolded:
India's Air Defence from WWII to Operation Sindoor
Author: Pankaj P Singh

ISBN: 978-93-49042-30-8

Published by:
JGS Enterprises Pvt Ltd
Imprint: The Browser | Fauji Days

Publisher's Address:
SCO 14-15, FF, Sector 8-C, Chandigarh 160 009

Website: thebrowser.org
Email: service@thebrowser.org

Printed in India

© Layout and Cover Design by beagles
99beagles.com

Publishers & Booksellers

Oral History & Military Publishing

Dedicated to our "Sentinels of the Sky"—the Corps of Army Air Defence—and all soldiers of the three services, not to forget the paramilitary and police, our defence scientists, and civil defence workers who together keep our skies safe.

Thank You!

CONTENTS

◆◆◆

Part II: The Interludes

Part III: India's Air Defence

PROLOGUE

◆◆◆

Operation Sindoor

◆◆◆

7 May 2025, 1.44 AM

A little while ago, the Indian Armed Forces launched *Operation Sindoor*, hitting terrorist infrastructure in Pakistan and Pakistan-occupied Jammu and Kashmir from where terrorist attacks against India have been planned and directed.

Altogether, nine (9) sites have been targeted.

Our actions have been focused, measured, and non-escalatory. No Pakistani military facilities have been targeted, and India has demonstrated considerable restraint in selecting targets and methods of execution.

These steps come in the wake of the barbaric Pahalgam terrorist attack in which 25 Indians and one Nepali citizen were murdered. We are living up to the commitment that those responsible for this attack will be held accountable.

—Ministry of Defense, GoI, on the PIB website

8 May 2025, 2.34 PM

On the night of 07–08 May 2025, Pakistan attempted to engage a number of military targets in Northern and Western

India, including Awantipura, Srinagar, Jammu, Pathankot, Amritsar, Kapurthala, Jalandhar, Ludhiana, Adampur, Bhatinda, Chandigarh, Nal, Phalodi, Uttarlai, and Bhuj, using drones and missiles. These were neutralised by the Integrated Counter-UAS Grid and Air Defence systems. The debris of these attacks is now being recovered from a number of locations that prove the Pakistani attacks.

Today morning, the Indian Armed Forces targeted Air Defence Radars and systems at a number of locations in Pakistan. Indian response has been in the same domain with same the intensity as Pakistan. It has been reliably learnt that an Air Defence system at Lahore has been neutralised.

Pakistan has increased the intensity of its unprovoked firing across the Line of Control using Mortars and heavy-calibre Artillery in areas in Kupwara, Baramulla, Uri, Poonch, Mendhar, and Rajouri sectors in Jammu and Kashmir.

—Ministry of Defense, GoI, on the PIB website

12 May 2025, Media Briefing

Briefing the media on *Operation Sindoor*, Lieutenant General Ghai and his Indian Air Force and Navy counterparts, Air Marshal A.K. Bharti and Vice Admiral A.N. Pramod, said Pakistan used a range of weapons—from Chinese-origin missiles and Turkish-origin drones to armed UAVs (Unmanned Aerial Vehicles) and loitering munitions—in its attempt to reach targets in India. Drawing a cricket analogy to explain the multi-layered, robust, integrated air defence systems in place, Lieutenant General Ghai said, "Targeting our airfields and logistics is way too tough.... I saw that Virat Kohli has just retired from Test cricket.... He is one of my favourites.... In the 1970s, during the Ashes between Australia and England, two Australian bowlers destroyed the batting line-up of England, and then Australia gave a proverb: 'Ashes to ashes, dust to dust, if Thommo don't get ya, Lillee must'. **If you see the layers, you will**

understand what I am trying to say. Even if you cross all the layers, one of the layers of this grid system will hit you."

Air Marshal Bharti said tri-service assets were deployed in a multi-layered system—point defence comprised low-level air defence guns and shoulder-fired weapons, while aerial defence comprised fighter aircraft and long-range missiles. A range of surveillance radars also formed part of the grid.

Lieutenant General Ghai said repeated attempts by Pakistan to target Indian airfields and logistics installations on 9 and 10 May were unsuccessful because of the robust air defence grid.

He said the first layer comprised counter-drone systems and MANPADS (Man-Portable Air Defence Systems), the second and third layer of the grid comprised point air defence, short-range surface-to-air missiles and medium-range surface-to-air missiles respectively. The fourth layer of the grid comprised long-range surface-to-air missiles.

According to Air Marshal Bharti, this complex counter-drone and air defence shield countered a range of Pakistani threats such as Chinese-origin PL-15 air-to-air missiles, Turkish-origin Yiha systems, aside from other missiles, long-range rockets, loiter munitions and a range of quadcopters typically used for surveillance. He said the numerous waves of drones and UCAVs used by Pakistan were also thwarted by indigenously developed soft and hard kill counter-UAS systems and well-trained AD personnel. "The IAF has put in place the most efficient and effective AD environment, by the Integrated Air Command & Control System (IACCS) of the IAF, which accords us Net-Centric Op capability."

He said older and battle-proven AD weapons like the Pechora, OSA-AK and the LLAD guns played a key role in countering the Pakistani threat vectors in the current operations and underlined the "stellar performance" of indigenous AD weapons like the Akash system.

...

Vice Admiral Pramod said the Navy was effectively using multiple sensors and inputs. "We are maintaining continuous surveillance to the degree our national interest may require or manifest, to ensure targeting at extended ranges."

"All these are conducted under the umbrella of a comprehensive and effective layered fleet air defence mechanism that caters for all threats, be it drones, high-speed missiles or aircraft, both fighters as well as surveillance aircraft," he said.

He said the fleet operates as a composite force, maintaining a surveillance bubble at extended ranges using advanced radars.

"Any target that is suspected to be a threat to either ships or installations or other assets is detected and identified using various identification systems, affording quick and clear distinction between commercial, neutral, and hostile aircraft or flying objects at ranges above the threat-perceived attack range," he said.

The Carrier Battle Group with its MiG-29 fighter air wing provides the first layer of this threat interception. He said helicopters in this mesh, having ASW roles, are equally equipped and highly capable of identifying and engaging both by day and by night. "In the current standoff, the presence of our aircraft carrier with a large number of MiG-29K fighters and airborne early warning helicopters prevented any suspicious or hostile aircraft close to the Carrier Battle Group within several hundred kilometres," he said.

The CBG, with formidable offensive capability, was able to operate with impunity and maintained an uncontested presence in the area of operations, he said.

"Effectively, it compelled the Pakistani air elements to remain bottled up close to the Makran coast, denying any opportunity to be a threat in maritime space," he said.

—Indian Express, National Edition, 13 May

Skyfall

◆◆◆

The first danger humanity ever knew did not rise from the earth—it fell from the sky.

Across cultures and centuries, the heavens have been as feared as they have been worshipped. In Indian thought, the sky is not void; it is Ākāśa, the primordial space through which light, sound, and fury travel. It is where Indra hurls his thunderbolts from atop his chariot; where Vritra, the dragon of drought, is slain, and the rains are released. The sky is divine, but it is also a theatre of violence.

When Arjuna fires the Agneyastra, a weapon of fire granted by the gods, the Mahabharata describes the sky lighting up as though dawn had broken in all directions at once. Ashwatthama's Brahmashirsha Astra, invoked in rage, is described as capable of burning the three worlds. Its fury is such that Krishna himself orders it withdrawn, fearing it will destroy unborn children and poison the earth. These are not metaphors. They are early visions of what we would one day call aerial bombardment, firestorms, and fallout.

Even in the Ramayana, Ravana's chariot rises above the clouds, and so does Rama's in return. Their duel is not bound to earth. It is celestial, airborne, devastating. The Vanaras build a shield with boulders and fire arrows into the sky. The battle is as much vertical as it is horizontal. The sky is a contested space—something to be mastered, not trusted.

◆◆◆

This idea runs like a current through the human imagination. In Greek mythology, the Titans wage war with Zeus, flinging mountains and hurling thunder from the heavens. In Norse lore, Ragnarök begins when the sky cracks open with a serpent descending from the clouds. In Chinese cosmology, the Sky Emperor rules not gently but through mandate and storm. Even the Judeo-Christian tradition warns of brimstone from heaven, angels with flaming swords, and trumpets that herald a sky-born reckoning.

Our literature carries this same ancestral tension. Shakespeare fills his tragedies with skyward omens—blood in the moon, stars falling out of line, thunder marking the turning of fates. In *King Lear*, the storm is both real and metaphorical, a reminder that nature, like justice, can come from above with terrible indifference. In *War and Peace*, Tolstoy describes the sky over Borodino as "low and leaden," a vault waiting to drop. In *The Iliad*, Zeus's aegis is a literal shield in the sky, dazzling and impenetrable, used to scatter armies below.

◆◆◆

And then there is modern war, where the sky is no longer symbolic. It is a source of real destruction, engineered and deployed. In the trenches of World War I, soldiers feared not the enemy before them but the gas and shells that fell from unseen aircraft. In the Blitz, children hid in cellars as bombs whistled through the London fog. In Hiroshima and Dresden, the sky did not just fall—it incinerated.

To this, we responded with stories and shields.

We built air raid sirens, not unlike conch shells warning of demon hosts. We wrote poetry under bombardment—Wilfred Owen, Keith Douglas, and Sahir Ludhianvi all tried to capture the silence that follows when the sky erupts. We imagined cities under energy domes, as in *Logan's Run*, *The Hunger Games*, or Black Panther's *Wakanda*. In *Star Wars*, planetary shields glow blue before being shattered. In *Star Trek*, the shield is always raised a second before catastrophe.

Even our gods carried protection from above. Vishnu's Sudarshan Chakra spins through the air, destroying from a distance. Shiva's

Trishula is hurled across time and space. The gods do not wait for the enemy to arrive; they intercept. The very concept of Shakti is as much a protective force as it is a destructive one—a shield that can flare as fire.

In Roman legions, the tortoise formation—the testudo—turned men into a living citadel, with shields layered above to resist aerial assault. That was tactical air defence without electronics, just discipline and design. In ancient China, mirrored walls were used to reflect fire arrows and dazzle archers. In medieval India, war elephants wore armour with curved crests to protect their heads from arrows dropped by invading cavalry. Even then, air defence was not abstract—it was a necessity.

When we lift our eyes upward, we remember what Chief Vitalstatistix feared and what every warrior knew: the sky is heavy. It can fall. And it must be held. Not by one, but by many. Not with hope, but with vigilance.

Chief Vitalstatistix (as featued in the Asterix Comic Strip)

Today, we call our shields by new names: Iron Dome, S-400, Patriot, Akash, Barak, and Arrow. But their purpose is the same as Indra's vajra or Ravana's chariot canopy. To see the sky before it strikes. To deny the gods their anger. To hold the heavens at bay.

And now, we build new shields not of iron but of code and cognition. AI (Artificial Intelligence) scans for drone swarms. Radars look beyond the line of sight. Satellites peer into the thermal shadows of launch. But for all our progress, the instinct is ancient: defend the space above, or risk losing the world below.

This book records that instinct. It is the story of how humanity has always feared the sky—feared its fury, envied its power, and ultimately tried to master it. From the first arrow to the hypersonic glide vehicle, from the dome over a walled city to the command node of a ballistic missile shield, air defence has always been more than hardware. It is a dream of survival.

◆◆◆

The sky has always threatened to fall. This is the story of how we refused to let it.

007

Tomorrow Never Dies

◆◆◆

Bond—Commander James Bond—never fired a surface-to-air missile. He never manned a radar station, nor stood at the helm of an anti-drone battery. And yet, no other figure in popular culture has done more to dramatise the invisible world of air defence—its anxieties, its technologies, its consequences—than 007.

Take *Skyfall*. At first glance, it's a deeply personal story. The ageing spy. The dying mother figure. The crumbling of old institutions. But look again, and *Skyfall* is about something much larger. The very title is a warning: the sky is no longer safe. It can fall. And when it does, it falls hard, fast, and without mercy.

In this world, enemies don't march—they drop. They're ex-agents gone rogue, yes, but they're also satellites hijacked mid-orbit, stolen stealth tech, cyber weapons launched invisibly into airbases. When M quotes Tennyson—"Though much is taken, much abides"—she's not just elegising a spy service. She's mourning the loss of an era when threats arrived on foot, not from above.

Bond's villains have always understood the sky. In *You Only Live Twice*, a mysterious spacecraft gobbles up others in orbit—decades before anti-satellite warfare became real. *Golden Eye* gives us a stolen electromagnetic pulse weapon, dangling in space and poised to wipe out command and control systems. *Moonraker* imagines laser-based air defence from space. It sounds absurd—until you realise DARPA

(Defense Advanced Research Projects Agency) has already tested the prototypes.

In *Die Another Day*, a solar mirror from orbit fires down on Earth, burning through tanks and airfields alike. And in *Tomorrow Never Dies*, the enemy sails a stealth ship, hiding from radar, staging a false flag airstrike to start a war. These are not coincidences. These are forecasts.

Across the Bond canon, we find a preoccupation with control of the high ground—whether that's the stratosphere, outer space, or the intangible ether of signals and satellite feeds. Bond may move through casinos, embassies, and car chases, but his real battlefield is always shaped by what's happening above his head. He's a ground-level response to sky-borne threats.

◆◆◆

More importantly, Bond films capture something deeper—the psychological dimension of air defence. That split-second decision when something appears on the screen and someone has to decide: is it a bird? A plane? A threat? Or nothing at all? Bond doesn't wait for the sky to fall. He reads the shadow before the storm. He pulls the thread before the missile launches. His world, like ours, lives on the edge of detection.

And if his villains constantly reach for the sky—controlling satellites, hacking drones, launching space-based weapons—it's because they understand the stakes. He who owns the sky owns the ground. That's not just a Bond plotline. That's doctrine.

So while James Bond never sat at an IACCS console or entered an air defence bunker, he understood its stakes. Through fast cars and sharp suits, he walked the blurred line between espionage and interception. And in doing so, he brought air defence out of the classified realm and into the cultural imagination.

◆◆◆

Sometimes, the most important stories about the sky falling aren't found in military manuals. They're found in the movies that teach us how much we stand to lose. And how much depends on seeing the threat before it hits the ground.

Mind Games

◆◆◆

Air defence doesn't just shoot missiles. It sends messages—some to the enemy, some to the nation itself.

There is a reason why this chapter is in the prologue here rather than the fag end after all the technology, history, and use cases. It is important we get this right.

◆◆◆

Air defence is, first and foremost, about its often-overlooked psychological and political dimensions—how it shapes public morale, diplomatic posturing, deterrence narratives, and even wartime psychology beyond the battlefield.

Nothing exemplifies this more than *Operation Sindoor*. Two nuclear-armed rivals played sophisticated mind games with each other, locked in a moment of high-stakes brinkmanship, turning their air defence grids into chessboards. While the jury may remain hung for a considerable time on the verdict, and reams will be expended, we should not miss the forest for the trees—it wasn't just a war of machines, but theatre played in the highest registers of fear and calculation. That it spilled over into absurd theatre on our television screens and our social media handles, with fake news and fake posturing flooding our digital lives, is only a testament to the societal impact and power of air defence.

Our minds were a part of the same chessboard as the drones, missiles, and fighters in the air.

◆◆◆

Air defence is typically portrayed as a kinetic system: radars, missiles, interceptors, and control nodes working in cold harmony to destroy incoming threats. But behind this mechanical precision lies a subtler battlefield—the one inside minds, cabinets, and newsrooms.

Air defence not only protects territory, it shapes perceptions—of strength, security, and control. For citizens, it can inspire confidence or panic. For adversaries, it can offer deterrence or provocation. For allies, it may signal stability or vulnerability.

Air defence, in short, is a political theatre, a psychological shield, and a strategic chess piece, all wrapped into a radar ping.

The Psychological Terrain of Operation Sindoor

When the Iron Dome intercepts a rocket over Tel Aviv, the emotional impact is as powerful as the explosion it prevents. Residents cheer the streak of interceptions. Footage circulates instantly, becoming morale ammunition. The state is seen not as just reacting, but preemptively protecting.

Contrast this with the helpless panic during air raids in Syria, where air defence was patchy and confidence was low, or the brief terror in Delhi during Balakot, when rumours of Pakistani retaliation led to sudden airspace closures and night-time flights being turned back.

Even when no missiles are launched, the visibility of air defence systems—on rooftops, near airports, or at VIP (very important person) rallies—reassures or alarms. This visibility is part of the design.

◆◆◆

So, for millions in India's northern belt, *Operation Sindoor* was not an abstract conflict—but a sensory event. People in Punjab, Jammu, Rajasthan, and Gujarat saw streaks of light cut across the darkness—interceptors tracing arcs, drones hovering like distant insects, fighter jets roaring in and out of blackened horizons. It wasn't a television broadcast. It was happening right then.

The psychological impact is not of trauma alone, but of displacement: the sudden knowledge that one's roof, one's sky, can no longer be counted on to protect. Towns like Poonch had to be evacuated after a number of residents died in cross-border shelling. Many families had their bags ready to move at short notice. Some were resigned to their fate.

People of the country who were away from the borders experienced it differently, safe in the knowledge that they were not at risk—yet.

◆◆◆

The first blackout wasn't announced. It just arrived—sudden, collective, and disorienting. Entire districts in Punjab and Jammu were swallowed in darkness, not because of power failure, but because of strategic silence. The government ordered lights out, fearing that illumination might guide enemy drones or cruise missiles toward their targets. But what it extinguished was more than electricity. It dimmed the very sense of normalcy.

In border villages, it became a ritual of fear: pull the curtains, douse the lamps, wait in silence. Children clung to elders. Phones glowed faint blue in courtyards. Rumours took on the texture of truth, passed from window to window in whispers. Every beam of torchlight felt exposed. Every flicker of a lighter was reconsidered. People no longer waited for news—they waited for the silence to break. Each sound in the air had to be deciphered: Was that thunder? A sonic boom? A missile? The sky became something to be feared, not trusted. But the blackout was not merely tactical. It turned private homes into bunkers, replacing control with vulnerability, and reminding people that they were now part of a battlefield they had not chosen.

There were strange ironies. Some families rediscovered old habits—candles, radios, and spoken prayers. Others sat in cars with the headlights turned off. Teenagers who had never known a power cut were confronted with a world lit only by fear and stars. Time slowed. Attention heightened. A bird flying at night could become a source of collective anxiety.

The blackout achieved what no siren could: it turned an entire region into a theatre of suspense, one in which every citizen was both audience and actor, alert not to what they could see, but to what they might hear next.

◆◆◆

Operation Sindoor was also fought through phones, televisions, and forwarded messages. Television channels went into overdrive. Studio maps of missile arcs and fighter movements flashed with dramatic urgency. Anchors speculated openly as jingoism merged with rumour. Some counted intercepts like cricket runs, others spoke of nuclear readiness. But in the flood of sound and image, something quieter was happening beneath the surface: a collective psychological unmooring.

On social media, the chaos intensified. Videos of airstrikes from other conflicts were shared as live footage from Rajasthan. A video game rendering of a missile launch made its way into a news broadcast. Old footage from Balakot, Gaza, and even Syria resurfaced with new captions. In WhatsApp groups, relatives forwarded unverified warnings: evacuations, radiation leaks, false alarms. The fear was not in the message. It was in not knowing whether to believe it.

The emotional effect was subtle but corrosive. People who lived far from the conflict zones—urban centres like Bengaluru, Mumbai, or Kolkata—felt closer to the war than those actually under fire. Anxiety rippled through group chats. Schools in non-border states issued alerts. Some began to stockpile groceries or medicines.

But the damage wasn't only about panic. It was about exhaustion. The emotional bandwidth of an entire population was stretched thin, caught between the overload of information and the poverty of clarity. Every image became suspect. Every silence became ominous. And amid the blur of real and fake, what people feared most was the possibility that they were the last to know something important. The war, in many ways, became a game of informational ambushes.

For those in border states, this was even more disorienting. The lived reality of drone sightings and shelling was being filtered, re-narrated, and sometimes distorted by people sitting hundreds of kilometres away. Disbelief crept in. "That didn't happen here," someone might say of a viral clip supposedly from their village. "That voice isn't even our dialect." And yet the image would continue circulating, gathering likes, outrage, and official silence.

The sky was contested. The ground was shaking. But perhaps the most pervasive combat zone during *Operation Sindoor* was the one between the ears, where truth fought fiction, calm fought frenzy, and the need to feel informed became its own form of vulnerability.

◆◆◆

Amidst the unfolding chaos, the Government of India, too, was communicating, messaging, and building not just a response, but a story. A story with symbols, with faces, with carefully chosen words—and one that carried a deeper message to its citizens—we are in control, we are composed, and this is not chaos.

The name itself—*Operation Sindoor*—was the first clue. Not metallic, not martial, not cold. But intimate. Cultural. Red. Sindoor is sacred. It invokes protection, sacrifice, and even the shadow of blood. In naming the operation so, the government reached for something deeper than military vocabulary—it evoked memory, emotion, and identity. This was not a mission about missiles. It was about defending the soul of the nation, as quietly and irrevocably as a streak of vermilion across a forehead.

Then came the briefings. Not by anonymous defence bureaucrats, but by Colonel Sophia Qureshi and Wing Commander Vyomika Singh—two highly competent, poised, composed women in uniform. This was no accident. Their presence said: this is a new India—professional, inclusive, steady under pressure. Their tone was clinical but calm. There was no warmongering, no wild speculation, no dramatic calls to arms. Just brief, precise updates: how many drones neutralised, how many airspace violations monitored, what remains under control.

And yet, within the restraint, a signal. A soft confidence. That India would not be baited into theatrical escalation. That the sky may be contested, but the ground of national composure would not be ceded.

The official messaging repeated three core themes: restraint, capability, and readiness. There was no room for triumphalism. No countdown clocks on state television. No dramatic footage from the front. The government knew the terrain was sensitive—not just politically, but psychologically. With two nuclear-armed neighbours exchanging fire and fakes flooding social media, the centre's messaging aimed to lower the volume, not raise it.

But beneath the official briefings, another current ran. The message was not just to the people—it was also to adversaries watching closely. By presenting a composed, decentralised, and well-networked air defence response, the government was saying: our shield works, our systems are fused, and we do not panic. Trust us, trust our shield.

◆◆◆

Conflicts like this don't end with ceasefires. They end with recalibration—of memory, of belief, of what it means to look upward and feel either awe or unease.

For the Indian public, *Operation Sindoor* is a turning point, transforming air defence from something distant and abstract—a military affair left to generals and radar rooms—into something felt, something seen, something shared. The sky is the narrative—lit up, cracking, speaking in frequencies once reserved for doctrine and war rooms, bleeding into WhatsApp chains and FM radio alerts.

For those in the border regions, the change is profound. Their skylines are the flashpoints. Their children have learned the difference between a fighter jet and a reconnaissance drone by sound. They now walk with a new knowledge: that proximity to a border also means proximity to a system—one that is working, yes, but also watching, deciding, sometimes faltering.

Elsewhere, across the cities and plains, the conflict has arrived as noise—filtering through the media, diluted by distance. And yet, even here, something has shifted. The idea of air defence is no longer a chapter in a civics textbook. It is a face now. A sound. A rhythm. The public's relationship with the military has become more nuanced—not just proud, but invested. People want to understand how these systems work. They want to know who mans the radars, who fires the missiles, who watches the sky when they are sleeping.

There is pride, yes. In the calmness of the response. In the silence of chaos. In the lack of spectacle. But there is also a new kind of vigilance. A recognition that security is not just about winning—it's about enduring. And that endurance, in the modern world, is as much about interception as it is about information, as much about command as it is about communication.

For the next generation, *Operation Sindoor* may become a story—like Kargil, like Balakot, like Pokhran before it. But unlike those, it will be a story about the sky, not the ground. About unseen threats. About systems that don't march, but hum. About war that feels less like a roar and more like a code running in the background of civilian life.

And in that story lies something quietly transformative. A new mythology, perhaps. One in which the old gods of fire and thunder have been replaced by domes, drones, and radar pulses. One in which the citizen no longer just worships the sky, or fears it, but learns to read it—pattern by pattern, echo by echo.

Because after *Sindoor*, the sky hasn't just returned to blue. It has become a question—like it already is in many parts of the world. And the people beneath it are learning to keep looking up—not in dread, not in awe, but in understanding.

Air Defence as Political Messaging

Nations use air defence deployments to send signals. When India deploys an S-400 battery near the China border, it is not just a tactical move. It is a geopolitical posture, signalling both deterrence and operational readiness.

When the U.S. (United States) sends Patriot batteries to Saudi Arabia, it signals a commitment to regional stability. When Turkey purchased the S-400 from Russia, it was a political rupture within NATO (North Atlantic Treaty Organization).

The purchase, placement, or even public discussion of air defence systems often becomes a foreign policy act. And in wartime? Their usage—or failure—can make or break international perception.

◆◆◆

Operation Sindoor has, similarly, sent a strong message to the international community. It was not just a shield but also a broadcast. And the message was calibrated with extraordinary precision.

India, through this operation, chose to speak in the language of restraint, but let that restraint carry the weight of capability. The very naming of the operation—*Sindoor*—was subtle and cultural, designed to signal internal resolve, not external aggression. It offered no hint of retaliation, vengeance, or escalation. Instead, it evoked protection, dignity, and the sanctity of what is worth defending. To the international community, this was a marked departure from the hyper-nationalist rhetoric that often accompanies border tensions elsewhere.

But beneath that soft tone was a strategic clarity: India was showing that it could absorb pressure without folding, manage escalatory risk with maturity, and conduct highly technical, layered air defence operations under real threat—all while remaining within the bounds of international law and proportionality.

The consistent deployment of uniformed women as the faces of official communication—Colonel Sophia Qureshi and Wing Commander Vyomika Singh—was a stroke of subtle diplomacy. It wasn't just about inclusion; it was with purpose. It projected India as a modern, gender-inclusive, professional military power, contrasting sharply with the image of adversaries still rooted in opaque hierarchies and bellicose posturing.

Furthermore, the government was acutely aware of who was watching. Washington, Moscow, Tel Aviv, Beijing, and capitals across the Indo-Pacific—all tuned in not just to what was happening, but to how India responded. The measured briefings, the nontheatrical tone, the absence of premature declarations—this was India auditioning for strategic credibility on the global stage. Not as a volatile nuclear rival, but as a nation with the temperament of a responsible regional stabiliser.

The operation also carried embedded messages for defence partners and suppliers. Every successful interception, every radar hand-off, every drone neutralisation was, in a sense, a live demonstration of India's growing military architecture—not just its imports like Barak or S-400, but its indigenous capability, its command and control systems, its operational discipline.

Of course, this strategy came with risks. Some foreign analysts interpreted India's composure as indecision. Others accused it of masking real conflict under the veil of strategic ambiguity. But these voices were largely peripheral. What mattered more was the overall reception: from most quarters of the international order, India emerged not as the trigger, but as the anchoring presence in a dangerous regional storm.

And that, ultimately, was the masterstroke of *Operation Sindoor's* international messaging: to respond with enough force to deter, enough control to reassure, and enough poise to be remembered.

When Air Defence Fails Publicly

Failure in air defence is never just technical. It's political.

The Mi-17 friendly fire incident during Balakot became a national concern—not just for its tragedy, but for what it suggested: confusion, fragmentation, vulnerability.

When Iran's AD (Air Defence) mistakenly shot down Ukrainian International Airlines Flight 752 in 2020, killing 176 people, it unleashed international condemnation, internal protests, and total loss of air defence credibility.

Such events don't just kill. They undermine deterrence, damage public trust, and give adversaries propaganda ammunition.

◆◆◆

Every war writes two stories: one for the moment, and one for history. *Operation Sindoor* will be no different. In real time, it played out in the skies, across command centres, on flickering television screens, and through cryptic press briefings. But as the smoke clears—literally and figuratively—it is but natural that the real contours of this operation will lie somewhere between fact and fog.

Both sides have claimed success. Interceptions tallied. Drones destroyed. Airspace violations thwarted. The numbers are there—but so are their shadows. Pakistan spoke of offensive superiority and radar penetration. India responded with a language of control and containment. And between these twin narratives lies a silent, shifting truth that neither side has fully revealed—and perhaps never will.

This is the nature of the fog of war: not merely confusion on the battlefield, but deliberate ambiguity in the information space. In *Operation Sindoor*, it manifested in timing lags, blurred footage, and carefully curated disclosures. Some radar tracks were made public. Others weren't. Certain interceptions were proudly broadcast; others were never mentioned again. In a conflict where both the defence and the deterrent were digital, kinetic, and psychological, success could be shown, exaggerated, or concealed with equal ease.

Even within India, assessments diverged. The truth is that no air defence system is invulnerable, just as no system is ever fully tested until the moment it fails. The significance of *Operation Sindoor* lies not just in the number of drones neutralised or threats intercepted, but in the stress test it imposed: on infrastructure, command logic, civilian resilience, and the very notion of strategic clarity.

India may rightly claim that it withstood an unconventional, multi-domain assault without tipping into panic or overreach. That alone is no small feat. But posterity will ask harder questions: Were there blind spots? Were there near-misses that never made it to press briefings? Did every protocol work as intended? And just as critically, what did the adversary learn from what we chose to show?

◆◆◆

Some truths will emerge in leaked after-action reports. Others in defence white papers a decade from now. Some will remain sealed in war diaries and encrypted communications. History has the patience to wait, even if politics and media do not.

What is undeniable is that *Operation Sindoor* proved India's air defence is no longer theoretical. It is active, it is visible, it is contested. But it is also evolving. The fog that hangs over the operation today is not just one of facts withheld, but of futures being shaped—in new procurement decisions, in reshaped doctrines, in drills rehearsed with new urgency.

The fog of war obscures. But it also reveals—slowly, and only to those who are willing to look through its haze without rushing to conclusions. What *Sindoor* achieved or failed to achieve will not be decided by today's headlines. It will be judged, quietly and precisely, by the silence of future skies.

The Deterrence Paradox

Air defence systems are no longer just tactical—they're strategic weapons. The presence of a system like S-400 or Iron Dome doesn't just stop an attack. It deters it altogether.

By deterring attacks, it raises the cost of action, encouraging adversaries to strike elsewhere or shift to non-traditional vectors (cyber, drones, information war).

But paradoxically, it may also provoke pre-emptive attempts to disable it (as seen in Iraq, Syria, Libya) and create a false sense of invincibility, leading political leadership to take bolder, riskier steps.

Thus, the perception of air defence strength must be carefully calibrated—not underplayed, not overstated. **Air defence has joined the nuclear triad, naval fleet, and satellite network as a pillar of national projection.**

◆◆◆

Where does India stand?

India sits at the intersection of three hard truths—its neighbourhood is armed, unstable, and unpredictable; its skies are wide, varied, and often exposed; and its defence budget, while large, is still stretched across multiple fronts.

Yet, despite these constraints, India has quietly built a credible, layered air defence framework. With the S-400 providing outer cover, indigenous systems like Akash and QRSAM (Quick Reaction Surface-to-Air Missile) forming the mid-layer, and Netra and IACCS tying it all together, India now has a functional, scalable air shield, which can act as a deterrent, too.

◆◆◆

Every military operation begins with a visible act and ends with an invisible question, as does *Operation Sindoor*. Did it work?

Deterrence is not about surviving one storm—it is about preventing the next. The stated strategic objective was clear: to signal to the adversary—and to the world—that India will not be found vulnerable, that attempts to do so will be met with smart, calibrated, and credible resistance, and that no low-cost asymmetric tactic (drone swarms, electronic jamming, glide bombs) will go unanswered or unanswered intelligently.

In this, the messaging was largely successful. Pakistan, after an initial flurry of bold claims, gradually shifted its posture—pulling back drones, dialling down radar provocations, and returning to familiar narratives of victimhood and restraint. China's reaction, while muted, included increased surveillance of its own border infrastructure. And most crucially, no further violations were attempted in the days immediately following *Sindoor*. The sky, in effect, became quieter.

But deterrence is never judged by silence alone. It is judged by the psychology of adversaries. Have their calculations changed? Do they now see escalation as too risky, or have they merely paused to regroup?

In this sense, *Sindoor* may have bought time, but not necessarily changed the game. The adversary tested India's response and found it disciplined—but also predictable. The absence of visible offensive counter-punches led some observers to ask: was the restraint strategic wisdom, or missed opportunity?

Internally, voices differed. Some veterans praised the precision and professionalism. Others quietly questioned whether the operation's termination was premature—cut short before a fuller degradation of the adversary's aerial launch platforms could be achieved. After all, deterrence is most effective when the cost imposed is not only visible but memorable.

Then there is the domestic political calculus. *Operation Sindoor* ended without a dramatic "mission accomplished" moment, without visuals of flaming wreckage or captured platforms. This may have frustrated some quarters, but it also underlined India's maturity in modern warfare, where optics are subordinate to outcomes, and restraint is not mistaken for weakness.

Ultimately, the real test of deterrence lies not in *Sindoor's* past, but in its aftermath. If the adversary now hesitates before launching another drone, if it begins recalibrating strike doctrines or dispersing command assets, if it seeks to avoid direct aerial confrontation, then *Sindoor* worked. If not, then it may have been an interlude, not a deterrent.

◆◆◆

What's certain is that India has raised the cost for the adversary. And that cost was calculated—not in megatonnage or megaphones, but in a steady stream of interceptions, the professionalism of its defence grid, and the quiet unity of its civilian posture.

Whether that cost was enough to change enemy doctrine—or simply to delay its timetable—only time, and future skies, will tell.

Public Morale and the Will to Resist

In prolonged conflicts, morale is as important as munitions. Well-integrated air defence, publicly understood and communicated, can give citizens a sense of agency (e.g., shelter protocols, siren drills), reduce panic and economic paralysis, and enable continuity of civilian life during conflict.

Operation Sindoor marked a critical shift in Indian civil-military psychology: for the first time, the air defence grid was not just protecting civilians—it was engaging them.

When sirens wailed in Ganganagar, residents knew which roads to avoid. In Jammu, families began referring to "alert zones" and "calm hours." Makeshift shelters, often improvised by local authorities in schools or *dharamshalas*, were quickly mapped and shared on neighbourhood WhatsApp groups. This wasn't the militarisation of society—it was the localisation of resilience.

Ukraine has shown this vividly: metro tunnels becoming safe zones, air raid apps becoming part of civic life, children drawing fighter jets alongside sunflowers. These aren't romantic gestures—they're functional responses that knit public morale into the broader security fabric. *Operation Sindoor* has begun that process in India, even if informally. The challenge now is to shape it, support it, and build systems around it—not for propaganda, but for readiness.

The goal isn't to create a bunker mentality. It's to ensure that in the next conflict, Indians know the sky may be contested, but the ground they stand on is not; that they are not just protected, but informed. When the Chandigarh Administration put out a call for civil defence volunteers during *Operation Sindoor*, no one expected a surge. The city, known more for its calm gardens than command bunkers, had rarely brushed against the immediacy of war. And yet, within forty-eight hours, the Deputy Commissioner's office was fielding thousands of registrations—many of them from students and young professionals. They didn't come to fight. They came to help.

All this will require investment—in public awareness campaigns, in city-level shelter protocols, in psychological and first-aid training, and in community resilience networks. But above all, it requires a new mental map—one in which air defence is not just a military shield, but a national state of mind. Because when the next warning sounds, missiles will matter. But so will milk vendors. So will teachers. So will those who hold the line not with weapons, but with routine.

◆◆◆

Operation Sindoor may have defended the skies. But its lasting gift may be that it taught a billion people how to stand steady beneath them. India, with its high population density and regional vulnerabilities, must build a civilian understanding of AD—not to militarise society, but to anchor resilience.

The Politics of Sovereignty

In diplomatic terms, air defence is territorial messaging.

Imposing a no-fly zone, activating a SAM (Surface-to-Air Missile) system, or closing airspace during a border standoff (as seen post-Balakot) signals political intent as clearly as a military buildup.

In India's case, partial integration of military AD with civil aviation ATC (Air Traffic Control) is still being refined—a gap that, if exploited, could have both military and political fallout.

In the modern world, where drones and missiles ignore borders but reputations do not, air defence is now a frontline of foreign policy.

◆◆◆

Air defence is not just a system. It is a story a nation tells itself—and the world.

A story of strength or confusion.

Of vigilance or unpreparedness.

Of resolve, restraint, or recklessness.

Every time a radar tracks an incoming object, it may do more than trigger a launch. It may trigger a signal—of deterrence, denial, or dialogue.

In war, the sky may belong to no one.

But the perception of who controls it may decide who wins on the ground.

PART I

THE WORLD OF AIR DEFENCE

What is Air Defence? How does it work? What is its history and future? UNFOLD the answers in this part.

CHAPTER 1

◆◆◆

Battlefields to Battlespace—The Birth of Air Defence

Once upon a time, war was horizontal. Soldiers marched, cannons thundered, and frontlines were etched into muddy earth. The sky was merely a canvas of clouds—beautiful, indifferent, unreachable. And then came the aircraft.

The first time a bomb was dropped from the air in combat was in 1911, during the Italo-Turkish War. It was a crude grenade tossed out by hand from a biplane over Libya. Nobody knew it then, but the sky had just become a war zone.

Fast-forward to today, and the idea of war without the air is unthinkable. Every modern battle—be it in Ukraine, Gaza, or over the Line of Control—is marked by a frenetic contest for the skies. Jets duel at Mach speeds. Drones buzz unseen. Missiles scream toward their targets.

And yet, for every weapon launched into the air, there is—ideally—a weapon waiting to bring it down. This is air defence. It is not just hardware; it is a philosophy. A promise that not every strike will land. That the sky, while still dangerous, can be watched, guarded, and defended.

What makes air defence especially fascinating is that it evolves with the threat. When aircraft first entered warfare, basic anti-aircraft guns tried to shoot them down. Then came faster jets—so we made faster missiles. Then came missiles—so we developed anti-missile missiles. Now we have stealth drones—so we use AI-powered radars.

Each new offensive invention is met with a new defensive counter. It's a game of cat and mouse, but in the sky—and with much higher stakes.

In war, victories are often seen. Air defence is the opposite. When it succeeds, nothing happens. No explosion. No fire. No headline.

But sometimes, it's dramatic. In 1991, during the Gulf War, CNN aired live footage of American Patriot missiles trying to intercept Iraqi Scuds over Israel. The explosions lit up the night sky. People cheered. Some missiles missed. Others hit. For the first time, the world watched an air defence system in action—and realised what it meant to defend the skies.

India had its moment, too, though quieter. After Balakot in 2019, Pakistani retaliation was met with Indian jets in the air, radar systems scanning every blip, and missile units on standby. It was tense. It was invisible. But it worked. And then came May 2025, when India launched *Operation Sindoor*. A conflict began where the air was not just a path for attack but a space contested, second by second.

◆◆◆

There was a time when a battlefield had boundaries. It was Normandy. It was Kargil. You could draw lines on a map and say: this is where the war is. But in the 21st century, war doesn't respect edges. It bleeds across dimensions—land, air, sea, cyber, and space—all at once.

The battlefield is, now, no longer a physical area. Instead, it is a "battlespace"—a literal architecture of conflict. Imagine a vast, invisible dome stretching across geography and time, where every entity—tank, submarine, radar station, drone, missile, satphone, or even a hacked CCTV feed—becomes a player. The enemy is no longer just a soldier or a plane; it might be a virus injected into your radar. Or a satellite jammed over Rajasthan. The battlespace is the grid, the network, that hum of signals in the ether. And somewhere in that hum, lives and nations hang in balance.

World militaries have been adapting to "networked" warfare for decades. The old-fashioned, seen-through-binoculars, two-dimensional, ships-soldiers-and-tanks battlefield suddenly got extended vertically all the way up to orbit and electronically well out into infrared and radar wavelengths—in which ubiquitous sensors pass targeting information to all sorts of "shooters" through seamless communication networks.

Hundreds of signals pulse through the sky—some encrypted commands, some live drone feeds, some radar sweeps, some jamming signals. In air operations centres, officers stare not at maps with pins and flags, but at dynamic screens filled with colour-coded arcs, blinking threat icons, and real-time telemetry.

> At precisely 0207 hours, a silent alarm lit up the corner of one such screen: Possible incoming: *Low-RCS object, altitude 1,500 ft, bearing 323.*
>
> It was likely a drone. It was not particularly fast, but perhaps loaded with enough explosive to flatten a fuel depot. And it was slipping through the gaps in the sky.
>
> The commander didn't reach for a walkie-talkie. He didn't shout. He tapped his console twice, sent the coordinates to the nearby SPYDER (Surface-to-air PYthon and DERby) missile battery, and watched as a dot on the radar screen was suddenly swallowed by another—blue overtaking red. Intercept successful. The battlespace remained quiet.
>
> Except, of course, it wasn't quiet at all.

Huge investments have provided the great powers, especially America and developed-world allies, with some of these wished-for capabilities. As General Mark Milley, America's top military officer, put it, "You've got an ability to see and an ability to hit at range that has never existed before in human history."

In this environment, it's not enough to be strong. You have to be aware—constantly. The real question isn't "Where is the enemy?" but "Who's watching the enemy watch me?" This complexity has given rise to a new doctrine: network-centric warfare.

The Web of War: Networked Combat

Think of it as the Internet of War. Every sensor, shooter, and decision-maker is connected. An artillery unit in Ladakh can receive coordinates from a drone flying over Bahawalpur. A radar station in Gujarat can cue a missile battery in Punjab. A fighter jet can "see" through the eyes of a surveillance satellite.

In such a system, data is the ammunition. Speed is everything. The loop—from detection to decision to destruction—must be tight, seamless, and error-free. Whoever loops faster, wins.

If the early hours of *Operation Sindoor* taught us anything, it's that India and Pakistan are now fighting not across trenches, but across grids. Battles are unfolding not just on runways or in missile silos, but in cloud servers, electromagnetic spectrums, and AI-augmented screens.

The defining stories are not just attacks launched, but attacks stopped, about systems that don't just fight but defend. About the unseen shield that hums in silence above us, holding off the war we never see.

But with so many eyes on the sky and so many hands on triggers, a new problem emerges: not every flying object is a friend. Not every signal is honest. How do you know what's coming? How do you stop it before it hits?

Enter the unseen but crucial player in this new game: Air Defence.

CHAPTER 2

◆◆◆

The Unseen Shield

> Victory smiles upon those who anticipate the change in the character of war, not upon those who wait to adapt themselves after the changes occur.
>
> —*Giulio Douhet, early air power theorist*

> To conquer the command in the air means victory; to be beaten in the air means defeat.
>
> —*Giulio Douhet, early air power theorist*

The moment a pilot lifts off the runway, he becomes a target.

The sky, for all its beauty, is the most hostile domain in modern warfare. It offers no cover, no trenches, and no shadows to hide in. Everything is visible—and vulnerable. Yet from this very sky, the most devastating strikes have originated. Think of Pearl Harbor. Think of the Twin Towers. Think of the cruise missiles that fly low and silently until they kiss their target with fire.

Now imagine a system designed not to strike, but to stop. To see through clouds and confusion. To calculate in milliseconds. To fire just once—and end an attack before it ever begins. That system is air defence. And in today's battlefield, it is no longer optional. It is the spine of national survival.

Air defence—or AD, as it is known in military shorthand—is the art and science of denying the enemy control of the airspace over your own territory.

◆◆◆

Air defence systems used to be like snipers: single guns watching single patches of sky. Today, they're more like goalkeepers in a hyperlinked stadium. The ball can come from anywhere—stealth drones from 30 feet up, cruise missiles from 300 kilometres away, or fighter jets flying nap-of-the-earth to avoid radar.

In the battlespace, air defence is not just a reactionary tool—it's an active node in the network. A radar sweep here adjusts a missile's guidance there. A satellite cue triggers a standby system underground. A drone's feed becomes targeting data for a man-portable launcher.

This is why air defence is not just about hardware. It is about being integrated—with radars, with command posts, with airborne warning systems, and with human judgment. Without this integration, even the most advanced missile is just a glorified firecracker.

To the untrained eye, it might look like a collection of surface-to-air missiles, anti-aircraft guns, radars, and control rooms. But in reality, **air defence is not a weapon**. It's a **process**—a tightly choreographed loop of sensing, assessing, and responding.

The goal is simple: detect what's coming, identify whether it's hostile, and neutralise it—before it causes harm. But the execution is anything but simple.

The Enemies in the Sky: Know Thy Threats

But what exactly are these threats that air defence systems are trying to intercept? They come in many forms—and increasingly, they don't look like planes at all:

Fighter Jets

The classic threat. Fast, manouvrable, and capable of air-to-ground and air-to-air attacks. Think F-16s, Rafales, Su-30MKIs. Their strength lies in speed and pilot intuition—but they're visible to radar and can be engaged if detected early.

Drones (UAVs)

From high-end armed drones like the Turkish Bayraktar TB2 to hobbyist quadcopters with improvised explosives, unmanned aerial vehicles are cheap, hard to detect, and swarming the modern battlespace. They're the new insurgents of the air.

Cruise Missiles

Low-flying, terrain-hugging missiles that sneak under radar and strike with pinpoint accuracy. The U.S. Tomahawk, Russia's Kalibr, or Pakistan's Babur all belong to this family. Slower than ballistic missiles, but much stealthier.

Ballistic Missiles

The big guns. Fired in a high arc, they exit the atmosphere and re-enter at tremendous speed. They're hard to stop and are often used to hit strategic targets. India's Prithvi and Agni, or Pakistan's Shaheen and Ghauri, are prime examples.

Hypersonic Weapons

Still emerging but terrifying—these travel at five times the speed of sound or more, manoeuvring unpredictably. Too fast for most traditional AD systems. Russia's Kinzhal and China's DF-ZF are already operational.

Loitering Munitions ("Kamikaze Drones")

A mix between drone and missile. They hover near the target zone and strike once a target is identified. Think Israel's Harop, or Iran-backed Shahed drones in Ukraine.

Electronic and Cyber Attacks

Not every strike is physical. Sometimes, the threat is a spoofed radar signal, a jammed communication link, or malware inside an air defence server. In a networked battlespace, disabling a sensor is as good as destroying it.

Each of these threats behaves differently and flies at different altitudes, speeds, and profiles. And each demands a different kind of response.

You can't fire a long-range missile at a balloon. You don't need a jet to take down a drone. You can't wait to identify a ballistic missile. So, modern air defence systems are layered—each layer designed to catch a different kind of threat at a different stage in its flight.

What Constitutes an AD System?

An air defence system is a networked combination of sensors, decision-making nodes, and interceptors designed to detect, track, identify, and neutralise aerial threats before they can inflict harm. It's not a single weapon—but a system of systems, often working across multiple layers and domains.

At its core, an air defence system includes:

Sensors (Detection Layer)

These are the eyes and ears, like radars (ground-based, airborne, shipborne), electro-optical and infrared sensors, acoustic sensors (for low-tech threats), and satellites (for ballistic missile tracking). They detect movement, measure trajectory, and determine speed and altitude.

Command and Control (C2) Systems

This is the brain of the operation, and includes C3I (Command, Control, Communication, Intelligence) or IACCS networks, human and AI operators who assess threats, decision nodes that classify targets and allocate weapon systems, and threat libraries and IFF (Identification Friend or Foe) protocols. This layer determines whether and how to respond.

Interceptors (Kinetic or Non-Kinetic)

These are the hands that act, consisting of surface-to-air missiles, anti-ballistic, and hypersonic interceptors, radar-guided anti-aircraft artillery guns, lasers, and RF (Radio Frequency) weapons for drones and small-scale threats, and jamming and spoofing tools for non-kinetic neutralisation (electronic warfare). Each is calibrated to strike at a specific altitude and range.

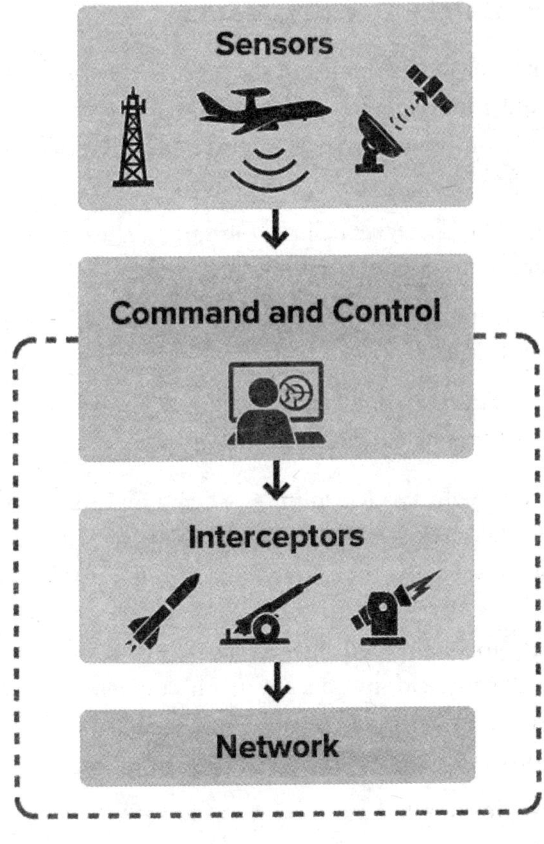

Air Defence System

The Network That Connects Them

The final and often most crucial component that provides seamless data links between sensors and shooters, real-time fusion of intelligence inputs from all services (air force, army, navy), and continuous feedback loops to assess whether the target was hit or escaped.

Together, these elements form what is often called an **Integrated Air Defence System (IADS)**. The integration allows a country not just to fire back but to fire smart, fast, and only when necessary.

Three Ds: Detect, Decide, Destroy

Every air defence operation, from the most advanced S-400 launch to the shoulder-fired Igla in a valley, follows a sequence as old as the first cave sentries: see danger, judge it, act fast. In military terms, this becomes:

Detect: Use radar, satellites, infrared sensors, or human intelligence to spot an incoming threat.

Decide: Is it a threat? What type? What path is it taking? How much time is left?

Destroy: Fire the appropriate weapon at the appropriate time, ideally with a single, precise shot.

This cycle might last ten minutes when a high-flying bomber is spotted 500 kilometres away. Or it might last ten seconds if a low-flying drone sneaks past the horizon. Speed is not just a luxury—it's life.

Contrary to Hollywood imagery, there's rarely a lone operator hitting a glowing red button. In truth, modern air defence is networked warfare at its most elegant. A single successful interception might involve:

An **early warning radar** detecting an anomaly 200 kilometres out.

A **satellite feed** confirming the trajectory.

A **command centre** analysing whether it's a decoy or real.

A **launch vehicle** tracking the object mid-air.

A **kill vehicle**—missile, gun, or drone—hitting the intruder before it reaches its target.

If even one node in this system fails—the sensor malfunctions, the radio link drops, the decision is delayed—the entire defence might collapse. That's why air defence is more like a symphony than a solo performance. Every instrument must be in tune.

Layers in the Sky

You don't build a wall in the sky. You build layers—a fortress, not with one gate, but with multiple concentric moats, archers, towers, and traps. That's how AD systems are designed. Each layer has a specific purpose:

Point Defence vs Area Defence: Whom Do You Protect?

In a dusty forward airbase near Jaisalmer, a lone Akash battery sits in wait. Its radar sweeps a wide arc of sky, its interceptor missiles primed. The base behind it houses fuel depots, command bunkers, and MiG-29s with tarpaulin covers. The job of this battery is not to protect the entire border sector. Its job is simple, sacred, and specific: protect this base. This is point defence.

Point defence systems are tailored for tight perimeters and high-value targets—airfields, command centres, ammunition depots, or moving VIP convoys. These systems react quickly, engage threats at closer range, and are often embedded directly into the asset they guard.

But step back a few hundred kilometres and you might find an S-400 unit with radars the size of billboards and missiles capable of intercepting threats 400 kilometres away. Its reach is continental. It doesn't protect just a base—it guards a region. This is area defence.

Area defence systems provide a strategic umbrella. They are slower to relocate, more complex to operate, and designed to intercept threats while they are still far from their targets—preferably over uninhabited ground. While point defence is surgical, area defence is sweeping.

The best defence networks, of course, combine both. One stops the arrow at the gate. The other intercepts it while it's still in the quiver.

Short-Range vs Long-Range: When Do You Fire?

The distance at which an air defence system engages its target is not just a matter of physics—it's a matter of doctrine and timing.

A short-range system like SPYDER or QRSAM is designed to react to what is already in motion nearby. These threats—low-flying drones, attack helicopters, even glide bombs—often appear with little warning. The missile's flight path is short, its warhead smaller, and the engagement window measured in seconds. Operators at these batteries often rely on visual confirmation, fast-track radar cues, and local command nodes.

On the other hand, long-range systems—like the S-400, THAAD (Terminal High Altitude Area Defence), or India's own upcoming XR-SAM (eXtra-long Range Surface-to-Air Missile)—are strategic weapons. They engage targets long before those targets can be seen with the naked eye. They watch the outer sky, scanning for ballistic missiles, high-altitude bombers, or cruise missiles flying nap-of-the-earth. These systems need precise early warning, complex data fusion, and longer decision loops. They don't protect one thing—they influence how the enemy flies, where it flies, or whether it flies at all.

The distinction, therefore, is not just about range—it's about pre-emption vs reaction, breadth vs immediacy, and deterrence vs survival.

Mobile vs Static: Will It Move with You?

When a convoy of Indian armoured units rolls toward a border axis, it's not alone. Somewhere nearby, concealed in a grove of acacia trees, a mobile air defence unit is tracking the skies, moving with the column, ready to deploy within minutes. This is mobile air defence—light, flexible, and combat-adaptable.

Mobile systems are crucial in fluid combat zones, especially for protecting advancing ground forces, forward operating bases, or high-value moving targets. Mounted on trucks, tracked vehicles, or even rail, these systems can "shoot and scoot"—firing at a target and repositioning before being detected themselves.

Contrast this with the radar dome atop an air force command post outside Agra. It hasn't moved in five years. It doesn't need to. This is static air defence—anchored to the terrain, often powering long-range systems with fixed infrastructure, hardened silos, and uninterrupted power supplies.

Static systems offer superior radar coverage, larger payloads, and more reliable command interfaces. But they are vulnerable to pre-emptive strikes and require layered support to remain survivable.

Modern doctrine increasingly favours a hybrid model: static systems for foundational coverage, and mobile units that can flex and surge when the threat shifts or advances.

Hence, an effective air defence network doesn't choose just one option from each category. It builds a matrix:

Long-Range AD: Intercepts threats hundreds of kilometres out (like the S-400 or THAAD). These are your "outer gates."

Medium-Range AD: Catches what slips through (like the Akash or SPYDER systems).

Short-Range AD: Shoots down targets in the last few seconds (guns like the L70 or MANPADS (Man-Portable Air Defence System) like the Igla).

Point Defence: Protects specific assets like airfields or HQs (headquarters) often using fast-reaction systems or mobile interceptors.

Each layer watches the other's blind spots. Together, they create what military planners call an Integrated Air Defence System, or IADS. Think of it as an aerial equivalent of overlapping body armour.

The Human Element

Despite automation, humans remain central.

A missile doesn't launch just because a blip appears. Someone has to confirm: Is it a hostile UAV? A flock of birds? A civilian airliner? Mistakes are expensive. During the Iran-Iraq war in 1988, a U.S. warship shot down an Iranian civilian airliner, killing 290 passengers—misidentified as a threat.

To prevent such tragedies, Rules of Engagement (ROEs) and Threat Libraries (databases of known flight signatures) are used. But ultimately, someone at a console must make the final call. Sometimes, that someone has five minutes. Sometimes, five seconds.

The OODA Loop: Thinking at the Speed of War

> In modern combat, it's not the bigger weapon that wins—
> it's the faster decision.
>
> *—Colonel John Boyd, U.S. Air Force, father of the OODA (Observe, Orient, Decide, Act) loop*

Picture a fighter pilot in the middle of a dogfight. The enemy is behind him. He sees a flash in his mirror—missile lock. He jerks left, fires flares, and banks hard. At that moment, his survival depends not on the size of his aircraft, but on a mental cycle he runs through faster than his opponent.

That cycle is called the OODA loop:

Observe: What just happened? What's in the sky?

Orient: What does that mean? Friend or foe? What's their angle?

Decide: Do I fire, flee, or feint?

Act: Do it. Now.

The OODA loop was developed in the 1960s by U.S. Air Force strategist Colonel John Boyd. He argued that all combat—whether between pilots, armies, or machines—boils down to this mental model. The side that completes its OODA loop faster than the other gains an edge. It stays unpredictable. It seizes the initiative.

Modern air defence is essentially about creating machines and systems that can run the OODA loop faster than any incoming threat—and in some cases, faster than human reflexes.

Radar observes. Computers orient. AI decides. Missiles act. It's not just war anymore. It's real-time choreography.

Sidebar: The Three Ds vs the OODA Loop

At first glance, Detect–Decide–Destroy might seem like just a shortened version of the more famous Observe–Orient–Decide–Act (OODA) loop. But while the two frameworks overlap in spirit, they serve different functions in warfare.

The OODA loop is about out-thinking your adversary. It's a mental and strategic model used by individuals, units, or entire militaries to adapt and respond to uncertainty. Fighter pilots in dogfights live and die by their ability to cycle through OODA faster than the enemy.

The Three Ds, on the other hand, are more mechanical and operational. They describe what a missile battery or radar station actually does when a threat appears:

You could think of the Three Ds as one short, lethal loop nested inside a larger OODA cycle. The missile doesn't strategise. It doesn't orient. It just executes. But the commanders coordinating these systems—watching the bigger picture—are constantly running OODA loops to outpace the adversary.

Or you could say that "Detect, Decide, Destroy" is the "Act" stage of an air defence system's OODA loop. OODA is about out-looping the enemy; the Three Ds are about intercepting the enemy. The Three Ds are tactical and technical—they are hardware-centric—

and describe how the machinery of air defence responds to an incoming aerial threat. OODA scope is cognitive and conceptual—it applies to individuals, units, or entire militaries—and is focused on outthinking and outpacing the adversary through rapid, accurate decision cycles.

The Cost of Invisibility

Here's the paradox: when air defence succeeds, nothing happens. The missile is intercepted. The drone crashes into an empty field. The plane turns away. There's no explosion, no body count, no headline. For the public, it's a non-event.

But for those in uniform, it's a quiet miracle.

During the 2023 escalation between Armenia and Azerbaijan, over 70% of the launched drones were intercepted by air defence systems. The casualty count, once expected to be in the thousands, stayed low.

This is the power of a working shield: to make war seem smaller than it really is.

In *Operation Sindoor*, India has already seen its skies lit with both threat and defence. Unmanned kamikaze drones, low-altitude missiles, and even decoy swarms have tested the country's network. Some were shot down. Some were not.

But every engagement sharpened the system. Improved the loop. Strengthened the shield. In modern warfare, winning isn't just about striking first. It's about stopping what comes next.

CHAPTER 3

◆◆◆

A (Very) Short History of Air Defence

No nation has ever built perfect air defences in advance of its first real air war. They've all had to learn on the job—sometimes too late, often at great cost. The history of air defence is the history of catching up with the sky.

The First Glimpse: Balloons and Biplanes

It began, as most military innovations do, with something that looked like a toy.

In 1794, during the Battle of Fleurus, the French army launched a hot-air balloon for aerial observation. It wasn't a weapon, but it triggered a chain reaction. If you could see from above, you could strike from above. And if someone could strike from above, someone else had to stop them.

The first actual air-to-ground bombing happened in 1911. Italian aviators dropped hand grenades on Ottoman troops in Libya from a biplane. Crude. Inaccurate. But symbolic.

During World War I, aircraft matured into serious war machines. Bombers flew over trenches. Recon planes mapped enemy positions. In response, ground troops fired rifles, machine guns, and even field artillery at anything with wings.

It was chaos. There were no dedicated air defence units. No radars. No doctrine. But the seed had been planted—control of the air now mattered.

World War II: The Age of the Gun and the Radar

If the First World War introduced air power, the Second turned it into a storm.

When the German Luftwaffe rained bombs on Warsaw, Rotterdam, and London, the British responded with a revolutionary invention: radar. Not only could it detect incoming aircraft, but it could do so before they were visible. This allowed Britain to scramble fighters in advance and conserve resources.

What followed was the birth of the world's first integrated air defence system—the Chain Home radar stations detected enemy bombers, the Ops rooms interpreted the data, and the Observer Corps watched with binoculars. Royal Air Force squadrons then vectored to intercept, while the Anti-aircraft guns (called "ack-ack") formed the last layer. It wasn't just hardware. It was a loop, a network, a system.

Meanwhile, in Germany and later the Soviet Union, massive anti-aircraft gun batteries filled the skies with shrapnel. Cities like Berlin and Moscow became fortresses ringed with flak. But even so, bombers still got through. Dresden. Tokyo. Hiroshima. The skies remained vulnerable.

The Cold War would try to change that.

Cold War: Missiles Replace Guns

After 1945, the new threat was not the slow, lumbering bomber—but the supersonic jet and, even worse, the ballistic missile. Anti-aircraft guns couldn't keep up. A shell had to be fired not where the target was, but where it would be—a near-impossible calculation at high speeds. So nations turned to guided missiles.

The Surface-to-Air Missile (SAM) was born—the U.S. introduced the Nike Ajax, and the Soviets followed with the S-75 Dvina.

In 1960, the world watched in awe when a Soviet S-75 shot down an American U-2 spy plane flying at 70,000 feet—thought to be untouchable. The age of the missile had arrived.

But with missiles came deception. Pilots flew low, fast, and erratically. In Vietnam, U.S. planes flew "wild weasel" missions—baiting enemy SAMs, dodging fire, and destroying radar sites. The hunter had become the hunted.

From Desert to Dome: Precision and Proliferation

The Gulf War in 1991 showcased the first televised air defence war.

Iraqi Scud missiles flew toward Israel and Saudi Arabia. American Patriot missiles rose to meet them. Some intercepted. Some missed. CNN broadcast it all live.

For the first time, the public saw how air defence was no longer a backroom affair—it was now theatre.

In the decades that followed, air defence systems became smarter—with better guidance systems, layered—combining long, medium, and short-range systems, and mobile—mounted on trucks, ships, and even backpacks.

Israel's Iron Dome became a household name after intercepting thousands of short-range rockets from Gaza. Russia's S-series (S-300, S-400) set the gold standard in area defence. The U.S. deployed THAAD and Aegis systems to shield allies in Asia.

But the threats also evolved. Cruise missiles flew below radar, and drones emerged—small, cheap, lethal. Swarms and decoys overloaded sensors. Hypersonics, too, appeared—too fast for most current interceptors. Air defence had won many rounds, but it was no longer a sure thing.

Lessons Etched in the Sky

Every major war since the Cold War—from Iraq to Syria, from Armenia-Azerbaijan to Ukraine—has served as a live laboratory for air defence evolution.

In Ukraine, for instance, the downing of Russian aircraft and cruise missiles by Western-supplied NASAMS (National Advanced Surface-to-Air Missile System) and IRIS-T (InfraRed Imaging System-Tail/Thrust Vector Controlled) systems showed how much could be done with the right coordination.

But also, it showed what couldn't.

No system, however advanced, has a 100% kill rate. No radar is omniscient. Air defence is a chess game played at Mach speeds. Every move teaches. Every mistake costs.

And Now, India

India's air defence journey began with British L70 guns and evolved through Soviet-era Pechora missiles, indigenous Akash systems, and now the acquisition of the formidable S-400.

But doctrine lagged behind hardware—until now.

With *Operation Sindoor*, the country has faced its most complex aerial threat scenario ever: drones, cruise missiles, and stand-off weapons, all used in coordinated waves. The system is being tested—not in drills, but in reality.

◆◆◆

What began with balloons and binoculars has now become a high-speed symphony of sensors, software, and steel. And India, like every modern power, must learn how to conduct it—or risk being overwhelmed by the noise.

CHAPTER 4

◆◆◆

Inside the System—How Air Defence Works

It always begins the same way.

A blip. A whisper on a radar screen. Not a roar, not an explosion. Just a flicker. Somewhere over a sector, a ground-based radar picks up something moving—fast, small, and headed east. The radar doesn't panic. It pings again. The object is now closer, traveling low, under 500 feet. Not a commercial airliner. Not a weather balloon. That's when the network comes alive.

In an underground control room, dozens of eyes lock on screens. Coordinates are cross-verified. The radar data is relayed to the Sector Air Defence Centre (SADC). An officer leans forward. Within seconds, he has to make a decision: is this a target—or a trick?

The system isn't just tracking a flying object. It's solving a puzzle in real time.

◆◆◆

Modern air defence begins with detection—a constellation of "eyes" watching the skies. Ground-Based Radars (GBR) scan long arcs of airspace from fixed stations, while Mobile Radar Units (MRUs) can be deployed to the frontline and hidden in terrain folds. Airborne Early Warning and Control (AEW&C) aircraft, like India's Netra, sweep massive areas from high altitudes.

Satellites feed thermal and visual data for long-range missile tracking. Even civil aviation data can be looped in to prevent fratricide. These sensors don't just see. They identify. Based on size, speed, trajectory, and radar signature, they compare every object against a threat database.

Some targets are known—like enemy fighter profiles. Others are unknown—like modified drones or home-built cruise missiles. And sometimes, the radar sees nothing at all—because the enemy is using stealth.

That's when the human mind takes over.

◆◆◆

Contrary to popular belief, air defence systems aren't fully autonomous—yet. At the heart of every potential interception is a decision-maker. Usually, a trained air defence officer sits in a command-and-control node. He's armed with information, but not certainty.

The question is rarely: "Can we shoot?"

It's usually: "Should we shoot?"

What if it's a decoy?

What if it's a civilian airliner flying off course?

What if multiple threats are incoming—which one first?

The answer depends on ROEs—rules of engagement—set by the military and government. Some systems can auto-engage low-risk targets like drones. But high-risk decisions require human clearance.

◆◆◆

Once a decision is made, the system transitions to its third D: destroy. The right response depends on the threat.

A slow drone might be downed with a shoulder-fired Igla, whereas a high-altitude bomber could trigger a long-range Akash or S-400 launch. Low-flying cruise missiles might be met by a SPYDER interceptor or even a burst of fire from a ZSU-23-4 Shilka.

The challenge is that most aerial threats travel at hundreds of metres per second. That means the missile must not just reach them—it must predict where they'll be. That's why interceptors often carry active seekers (radar or infrared) to course-correct mid-flight. The goal is either to explode near the target (proximity kill) or hit it head-on (direct kill).

An ideal intercept happens outside the defended area. But when it doesn't, point defence systems step in—firing last-minute shots, even at the doorstep of airbases and cities.

◆◆◆

Behind every shot fired is a network of links. In military terms, this is called the kill chain.

Find the target

Fix its location

Track its path

Target the best response

Engage with force

Assess the result

In older systems, this chain was slow and manual. Today, it's digital, high-speed, and spread across a layered defence grid.

◆◆◆

India's current AD architecture includes:

S-400 systems for long-range interception.

Akash and SPYDER for medium-range engagements.

Quick Reaction Surface-to-Air Missiles (QR-SAMs) on mobile launchers.

Anti-aircraft artillery near key installations.

AEW&C aircraft and integrated C3I (Command, Control, Communication & Intelligence) grids connecting it all.

The moment a threat is detected, the system allocates which node should intercept. It's like an orchestra assigning each musician their cue—except the music is war.

If the intercept fails, alerts ripple across the grid. Other nodes prepare for follow-up. Ground troops are warned. Civil defence is alerted. Fallback procedures are activated—hardened shelters, signal blackouts, or scrambling of fighter jets.

If the intercept succeeds, the data is harvested. Did the missile respond to commands correctly? How close was the hit? What was the flight path of the incoming threat? Can it tell us something about the enemy's tactics? Every success is analysed. Every failure is studied harder.

◆◆◆

Air defence has no luxury of failure. A single leak in the sky can mean a dead battalion. Or a cratered runway. Or a hospital in ruins.

Unlike other military systems, AD must perform not in peacetime practice, but in wartime pressure. When threats are layered. When signals are jammed. When deception is everywhere. In *Operation Sindoor*, Indian AD crews have had to deal with drones flying low under radar beams, swarms of decoys launched to mask real missiles, and GPS (Global Positioning System) spoofing attacks trying to disorient launchers.

And yet, the shield has held—for the most part. Every successful intercept has bought time. Every miss has brought urgency. Because war, in the end, is not won just by offence. It's often survived by defence.

CHAPTER 5

◆◆◆

Anti-Aircraft Artillery—The OG Air Defence

By the time of World War I, aircraft had evolved from curious machines into tools of reconnaissance, and then weapons. They dropped bombs from open cockpits, strafed trenches, and shattered the presumed invulnerability of static defence.

The first reaction was improvised: machine guns bolted to wagons, turned skyward in hope rather than certainty. But soon, artillery adapted. The war saw the birth of the Flugabwehrkanone, or Flak gun—the first true anti-aircraft (AA) artillery, developed by the Germans. These guns were designed to fire exploding shells into the air with timed fuses, creating shrapnel clouds in the flight path of enemy aircraft.

It was no longer about hitting the plane—it was about making the sky itself hostile.

Between the Wars: Theory and Trajectory

In the interwar period, militaries began formalising anti-aircraft doctrines. The British developed mobile AA units with searchlights. The Germans refined predictive firing tables—manual calculations of altitude, speed, and angle to increase hit probability.

But the biggest challenge remained: how do you hit a fast-moving aircraft with a shell that takes seconds to reach its altitude? The solution came in the form of gun directors and analog computers—devices that tracked aircraft and calculated the exact fuse timing needed to explode near the target. These primitive "brains" laid the groundwork for future fire control systems.

World War II: The Age of Flak

The Second World War was the golden age of the anti-aircraft gun.

The German 88mm Flak 36 became legendary—not just for downing Allied bombers, but also for its secondary role as an anti-tank weapon. These guns formed walls of steel over cities like Berlin, with entire flak towers rising from the ground, bristling with guns and spotlights.

The Allies responded with their own Bofors 40mm guns, used by the British and Americans, that were compact, mobile, and ideal for low-altitude defence, and the U.S. 90mm M1 AA gun formed the backbone of strategic defence against high-flying threats.

Cities like London, Hamburg, and Tokyo pulsed with the rhythmic boom of AA fire. And yet, despite their ferocity, only a small percentage of AA shells ever brought down aircraft.

Victory lay not in precision, but in deterrence—forcing bombers higher, wider, and less accurate.

Korea and Vietnam: The Gun vs the Jet

With the jet age, aircraft began to outrun the guns. But anti-aircraft artillery didn't disappear—it evolved.

In Korea, AA guns were still effective against low-flying aircraft, helicopters, and slow-moving bombers.

In Vietnam, the North Vietnamese employed massive volumes of Soviet-supplied AA guns—from 14.5mm machine guns to 57mm and 100mm radar-guided cannons—to lethal effect. U.S. pilots often found themselves flying through layers of fire, where speed and altitude alone no longer guaranteed survival.

The solution? Guns became smarter.

The Digital Gun: Radar and Automation

From the 1960s onward, AA guns began integrating with radar fire-control systems, removing guesswork from targeting. One of the most effective systems born from this integration was the ZSU-23-4 "Shilka"—a Soviet self-propelled AA gun mounted with four 23mm cannons and a target-tracking radar.

ZSU-23-4 Shilka (Courtesy: Wikipedia)

Nicknamed "the Sewing Machine" by NATO pilots for its high-pitched fire, the Shilka was mobile, fast, and deadly against low-flying threats.

Other nations followed. The U.S. developed the M163 Vulcan Air Defense System, using a 20mm Gatling gun, while the British deployed radar-assisted Marksman turrets.

Naval vessels began mounting Close-In Weapon Systems (CIWS) like the Phalanx, capable of firing 4,500 rounds per minute, using radar to track and destroy incoming missiles.

AA guns were no longer just defensive—they were automated terminators, designed to be the last line of defence when everything else failed.

The Gun Today: Against Drones and Missiles

In the age of hypersonic missiles and long-range SAMs, do guns still matter?

Yes—now more than ever.

In urban warzones, like Syria or Ukraine, AA guns are used to intercept drones, provide ground fire, and operate in GPS- or radar-denied environments.

In India, L-70 Bofors guns, though decades old, have been upgraded with digitised fire control radars and electro-optical tracking, making them relevant against low-cost aerial threats.

India's indigenous VSHORAD (Very Short Range Air Defence) systems and mobile ZSU Shilka upgrades are now being used to protect bases and convoys against loitering munitions and swarm drones.

The gun has returned to relevance by adapting—not by outrunning the missile, but by aiming where the missile doesn't: low, slow, and sudden.

LEGACY VS MODERN GUN-BASED AD SYSTEMS

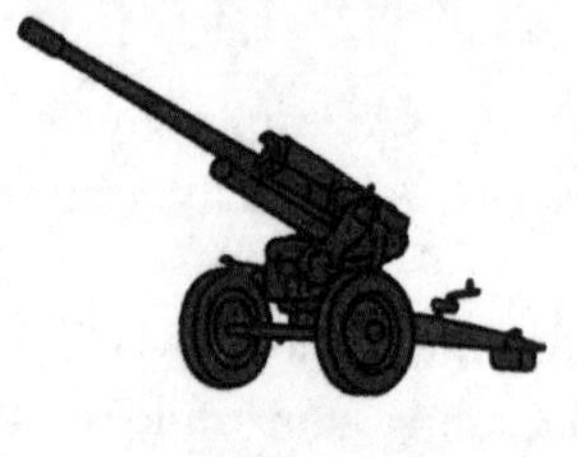

LEGACY

- Manual Aiming
- Optical Sights
- Trailed Platform

MODERN

- Radar-Guided
- Electro-Optical Sensors
- Self-Propelled

A Philosophy of Resilience

Missiles are fast, final, and expensive. But guns? Guns are persistent. Guns are patient. Guns don't run out as quickly.

They're often the first to fire when radars see something unexpected, and the last to stop when missiles have missed or run dry.

In the grand architecture of air defence, guns may no longer be the stars. But they are still the anchors—a reminder that sometimes, when all else fails, it is the old rhythm of steel and smoke that stands between sky and ruin.

CHAPTER 6

Radar—The Beating Heart of Air Defence

Without the radar, there would have been no meaningful air defence. not in 1940, and not in 2025. Radar has always been, and remains, the beating heart of every serious air defence system.

Before radar, air defence was guesswork. Early anti-aircraft guns in World War I and the interwar years fired into the sky based on visual sightings, crude acoustics, or even mathematical prediction tables. The success rates were dismal.

Then came the Chain Home radar network in Britain during World War II. When the Luftwaffe attacked in the Battle of Britain, radar gave the Royal Air Force minutes of early warning—enough to scramble interceptors, direct anti-aircraft fire, and conserve resources. It turned the tide. In a very real sense, radar saved Britain.

Even in today's networked, AI-assisted, missile-saturated battlespace, radar remains irreplaceable for three reasons:

Detection at Range: Radar is still the primary means of detecting aerial threats hundreds of kilometres away—be it aircraft, cruise missiles, or ballistic targets.

Target Tracking and Discrimination: Advanced radars don't just see—they classify. They can distinguish between a decoy drone and a real warhead, between a weather balloon and a stealth jet.

Cueing the Kill Chain: Every part of the Three Ds—Detect, Decide, Destroy—starts with radar. Without it, missile batteries are blind, and command centres are guessing.

Even new technologies like infrared search-and-track (IRST) or passive sensor networks only complement radar. They do not replace it.

A History of Radar in Air Defence

On a damp spring morning in 1935, in a windswept field outside Daventry, England, a small team of British scientists aimed a radio beam toward the sky. Their equipment was crude—cables snaked across the grass, valves buzzed faintly—but their results were revolutionary.

As an RAF bomber flew through the beam's invisible arc, the instruments registered a faint disruption. The airplane had bounced back the radio waves.

Sir Robert Watson-Watt, the Scottish physicist leading the experiment, turned to his assistant and said something that would enter legend: "Gentlemen, this is the direction from which the enemy will come."

That experiment would birth what we now know as radar—Radio Detection and Ranging—and with it, the dawn of modern air defence.

◆◆◆

Just five years later, Britain faced annihilation.

The Luftwaffe, under Hermann Göring, launched waves of bombers toward England in what became known as the Battle of Britain. For the first time, a nation was under siege not by invading troops, but by an airborne armada.

But Britain had an edge.

It had built a secret network of radar stations along its southern coast—Chain Home. These massive, skeletal towers looked like crude scaffolding, but they held a secret power: they could detect incoming aircraft up to 120 miles away.

Every morning, the RAF Fighter Command would receive radar plots: height, heading, and speed of German formations. Commanders used this information to scramble fighters exactly when and where needed, conserving aircraft and fuel.

Winston Churchill later wrote: "Never in the field of human conflict was so much owed by so many to so few." But what most people forget is that those few never flew blind. They had radar.

◆◆◆

Early radars like Chain Home were large, fixed, and limited in range and resolution. But wartime necessity accelerated innovation.

The Germans, meanwhile, developed the Würzburg radar, a dish-shaped unit used to direct anti-aircraft guns. The Americans invented SCR-584, a portable radar that could track enemy planes and even guide gunfire using analog computers.

By 1944, radar-directed flak towers in Berlin were so accurate that Allied bombers often had to fly at suicidal altitudes just to get through. The radar had become not just a scout—but a weapon's guide.

Cold War and the Rise of the Missile

After World War II, the jet age began. Aircraft became faster, deadlier, and could now drop nuclear bombs. Suddenly, detecting a formation at 80 miles wasn't enough. Minutes mattered.

In the U.S., the threat of Soviet bombers prompted the creation of SAGE (Semi-Automatic Ground Environment)—an enormous computer-based radar system that spanned the country and could vector interceptors automatically.

Meanwhile, the Soviet Union developed radar-guided SAM systems like the S-75 Dvina, which famously shot down U-2 spy plane pilot Francis Gary Powers in 1960. That kill was a radar-guided strike. A slow-flying plane at 70,000 feet was no longer safe.

Air defence had entered the missile era, and radar had evolved from early warning to target tracking and missile guidance.

◆◆◆

In Vietnam, American fighter pilots encountered a new terror: radar-guided missiles launched from hidden SAM sites. The telltale "beep" in their cockpit meant one thing: they were being painted by radar, and a missile was likely on its way.

Pilots adapted. They flew low. They jammed frequencies. They developed SEAD (Suppression of Enemy Air Defence) missions, using "Wild Weasel" aircraft to bait SAMs into switching on their radar—and then destroy them.

Meanwhile, in the Yom Kippur War of 1973, Israel suffered heavy losses flying into Egyptian airspace protected by a Soviet-style radar net. Only after deploying jammers and developing better anti-radiation missiles did they begin to blunt the radar-driven defence.

These wars proved that radar wasn't just helpful—it was the pivot point of the aerial battlespace.

Radar Becomes Intelligent

By the 1980s and 1990s, radar had transformed. The old rotating dishes were giving way to phased-array radar, where beams could be steered electronically, not physically. These radars could:

Track multiple targets simultaneously.

Guide multiple interceptors.

Switch frequencies to avoid jamming.

Detect stealthier, lower-RCS targets.

One example: the AN/MPQ-53 radar used in the Patriot missile system, which tried (and sometimes succeeded) in intercepting Iraqi

Scuds during the 1991 Gulf War. Radar was no longer a watcher. It was a battlefield conductor, orchestrating the kill chain.

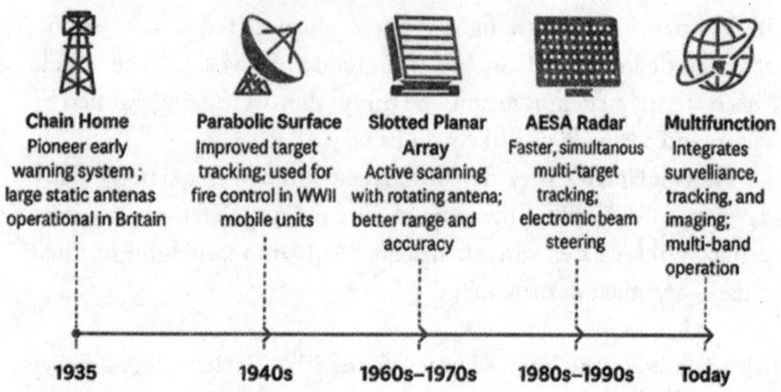

Today: The Radar Web

Today's radar systems in air defence are multi-band, multi-role, and multi-domain.

India's IACCS relies on a network of long-range surveillance radars (like the Israeli EL/M-2084), height-finders, and fire-control radars that guide missiles like Akash and S-400. AEW&C aircraft, such as India's Netra, provide 360° radar coverage from the sky.

Modern radars can now detect stealth aircraft by their minute turbulence trails and swarming drones by their collective movement signatures. Even hypersonic missiles are picked up using multi-frequency waveforms and predictive algorithms.

They are assisted by AI-based threat classification, fused data from satellites, and cross-domain integration. And yet, the core principle remains unchanged from 1935: send a wave, receive a signal, and see what can't be seen.

Radar's Vulnerabilities and the Next Phase

But radar is not invincible.

Jamming and spoofing can confuse or blind it. Anti-radiation missiles home in on radar emissions to destroy them, while cyber attacks can disrupt radar command networks. Also, stealth technology continues to challenge radar's limits.

The response? Silent radars, passive radar networks, and multi-static arrays—where transmitters and receivers are placed at separate locations, making them harder to target.

India is now investing in such next-gen radar ecosystems, including the Uttam AESA (Active Electronically Scanned Array) radar and radar satellites under ISRO, and integrating civilian air traffic sensors for layered situational awareness.

◆◆◆

From a chain of scaffolding towers in southern England to a digitised dome over the subcontinent, radar has not just evolved—it has endured.

It has adapted with every leap in aviation, every missile breakthrough, and every stealth innovation.

In the world of air defence, a missile without a radar is blind. A battery without a radar is deaf. And a nation without radar is dreaming, not defending.

CHAPTER 7

◆◆◆

Missile—The Clenched Fist of Air Defence

If radar is the beating heart of air defence, then the missile is its clenched fist—the striking arm that delivers the final blow.

Where radar sees, tracks, and warns, the missile acts. And the story of air defence is not just about watching the sky, but about reaching into it—fast, far, and decisively. From its wartime origins as a desperate gamble to today's precision interceptors that thread a needle at Mach speeds, the air defence missile has become one of the most dynamic weapons of the modern age.

The Second World War proved that the sky had become a deadly theatre. Bombers flew faster, higher, and in greater numbers than ground fire could manage. Even with radar telling gunners where to aim, the chance of hitting a fast-moving aircraft with a shell was brutally low.

The Allies tried everything—from proximity fuses to flak corridors—but none was perfect. Then came the idea: what if you could fire a projectile that could steer itself toward the aircraft?

This was the birth of the guided missile.

The Germans got there first. Their Wasserfall surface-to-air missile (SAM), built in the 1940s, never made it to operational use, but it showed the concept worked: radio-command guidance, radar tracking, and a vertical launch.

But it was the Cold War that turned the concept into doctrine.

Cold War: The Missile Joins the Orchestra

In 1953, the Soviet Union introduced the S-25 Berkut, the first operational air defence missile system—deployed in concentric rings around Moscow. It was massive, complex, and designed to stop American B-52 bombers.

But it was the S-75 Dvina (SA-2 Guideline) that changed history. On 1 May 1960, the Soviets used it to shoot down a U.S. U-2 spy plane piloted by Francis Gary Powers at 70,000 feet. Until that moment, the world believed such high-altitude aircraft were untouchable. The S-75 proved otherwise.

The message was clear: if radar was the eye, missiles were the hand—and the hand could now reach the heavens.

◆◆◆

The Americans responded with their own missile defences. The Nike Ajax and later Nike Hercules guarded U.S. cities. The Hawk system became a backbone for field-level air defence. The arms race was on—not just in nukes, but in who could stop what flew.

During the Vietnam War, the S-75 returned, now in Vietnamese hands. U.S. aircraft flying bombing missions over Hanoi began falling from the sky, hit by radar-guided missiles that rose without warning.

The missiles didn't need to be accurate—they just needed to explode near their target. And they did. Over and over again.

To survive, U.S. pilots developed new tactics. They flew nap-of-the-earth to avoid detection, used chaff and jammers to confuse missile guidance, and launched "Wild Weasel" missions—aircraft that hunted radar stations before missiles could launch.

The missile had transformed air defence into a deadly chess game, where every launch revealed a position, and every success taught the enemy how to adapt.

◆◆◆

In 1973, during the Yom Kippur War, Israeli pilots flew into a death trap.

Egypt had created a SAM umbrella—a dense network of mobile Soviet-made SAM batteries, including the SA-6 "Gainful". Israeli aircraft were denied freedom of the air—something that had never happened before.

Dozens of Israeli jets were downed. It was one of the few times in history when air defence shaped the outcome of ground operations.

Eventually, Israel adapted by developing new precision-guided weapons and electronic warfare units—but the missile had proven its role. The sky could now be contested.

The Gulf War: Patriot vs Scud

By 1991, the air defence missile had become a celebrity.

Iraq fired Scud missiles at coalition bases and Israeli cities. The U.S. responded with Patriot missiles, attempting real-time intercepts over live TV. Some worked. Some didn't.

But the world was watching, and the missile became the symbol of a defensive will—not just to strike, but to protect.

◆◆◆

The post-war years brought more advanced missiles. THAAD (Terminal High Altitude Area Defence) is designed to catch ballistic missiles in space. Aegis SM-3 interceptors can be launched from U.S. Navy ships. India's Akash and S-400 systems are capable of a layered, radar-guided response.

The Missile Learns to Think

Today's air defence missiles are not mere rockets. They are smart, guided, often AI-assisted machines.

They use active radar seekers that lock onto targets after launch and infrared homing to hunt down stealthy or low-flying targets. Networked guidance is in place where launch and kill don't have to come from the same unit.

Some, like the Iron Dome's Tamir missile, even calculate the impact point of incoming rockets and choose to intercept only if civilians are at risk. Others, like India's Barak-8 or Russia's S-500, can engage multiple targets simultaneously—jets, cruise missiles, and drones.

And yet, the principle is timeless: "Something is coming. It must be stopped. Launch."

Hypersonics

The missile is now facing its own limits. In the world of air defence, there has always been a moment—a sliver of time—between detection and response. That gap, however thin, has been enough. Enough to launch a missile. Enough to scramble a fighter. Enough to react. But with the advent of hypersonic weapons, that moment is disappearing. The very idea of reaction time is being rewritten.

Hypersonic weapons are too fast for many current systems. Defined as those travelling at speeds above Mach 5, they have moved beyond the realm of prototype and into active arsenals. Russia's Kinzhal and China's DF-ZF are not speculative projects; they are operational weapons capable of outpacing not just interceptors, but decision-making cycles themselves. At such speeds, a missile can cover a thousand kilometres in under ten minutes. And these aren't mere fast-moving projectiles. Many hypersonic systems are manoeuvrable mid-flight, flying at altitudes that dodge traditional radar envelopes—too low for space-based sensors, too high for conventional ground radars. They twist through the sky like fire without a trail, appearing on the screen only when it's far too late.

The implications for air defence are profound. The old playbook—detect, track, launch, intercept—is breaking down. Traditional radar arrays, even the most advanced phased-array systems, struggle to see these weapons coming in time. And even if they do, current-generation interceptors lack both the speed and the agility to catch them. It's not just a technological problem. It's a doctrinal one. Air defence systems are built around time: time to analyse, time to act, time to update. Hypersonics deny all three.

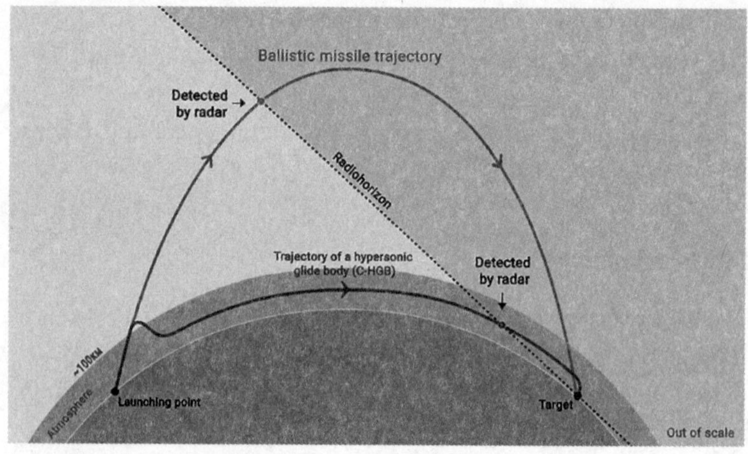

Comparison of Ballistic Missile and Hypersonic Glide Vehicle (C-HGB) Flight Trajectories (Courtesy: Wikipedia)

In response, nations are racing to develop a new ecosystem of sensors and decision networks. Infrared satellites with global coverage, low-earth-orbit radar constellations, and AI-assisted target discrimination are becoming the front line, replacing human decision-makers in the earliest moments of detection. Space-based early warning systems, long the backbone of strategic missile defence, are being redesigned to detect heat trails from hypersonics at launch. The sensor gap is moving upwards and outwards, into the stratosphere and beyond.

India, too, is entering this domain. Its Hypersonic Technology Demonstrator Vehicle (HSTDV) tests signal not just offensive ambition but also defensive necessity. Because in a world where missiles fly faster than thought, the only real defence may be to know before anyone else does—to see a launch before it becomes a threat, and to respond before the sky goes silent.

Along with hypersonics, there are other challenges as well—drone swarms are too numerous to intercept affordably, lasers and railguns that are being developed to fire at the speed of light, not Mach 3, and others.

Still, even with futuristic tools, the missile remains indispensable. It is still the best, fastest, and most deployable way to deliver lethal energy to a threat in the air. A single interceptor, launched in time, can change the fate of a city.

The missile in air defence is more than a projectile. It is a decision. Once launched, it does not return. It is the embodiment of certainty. It must know its target, find it, and kill it—often in seconds, under pressure, against a moving enemy who is trying to kill you first. It is the most disciplined form of violence the modern world has invented.

CHAPTER 8

◆◆◆

Interceptors—The Sword Arm of Air Defence

If the radar is the heart, and the missile the clenched fist, then the interceptor is the sword—wielded, not launched, and able to feint, parry, or strike with precision and intelligence. It is the defender's blade held in reserve, guided by a living mind, honed for speed, reach, and discretion.

Unlike the missile, which commits irreversibly once fired, the interceptor can approach without destroying, observe without engaging, and strike only when the judgment aligns with necessity. It offers not just protection, but the possibility of choice in a battlespace defined increasingly by automation and irreversibility.

They are the first to scramble, the last to disengage, and in many countries, they remain the only viable counter to threats that fly low, change direction, or appear unexpectedly over terrain that blinds radar.

◆◆◆

The interceptor's role was born in the shadow of the strategic bomber. In the 1930s and '40s, when air raids were first used to decimate cities, countries began building fast, lightweight fighters not just for dogfights—but to intercept bombers before they reached targets.

In the Battle of Britain, Supermarine Spitfires and Hawker Hurricanes rose from grass runways to meet swarms of German bombers over the Channel. Radar gave the warning, but it was interceptor pilots who made the kill. They were guided, not dispatched blindly.

◆◆◆

In the Cold War, this role became codified: interceptors like the American F-106 Delta Dart, Soviet MiG-25, and British Lightning were designed for one job: scramble fast, climb high, kill quickly.

How Interceptors Differ from Fighters

While all interceptors are fighters, not all fighters are interceptors. The interceptor is typically optimised for high-speed climb and straight-line pursuit.

They are equipped with long-range radars and air-to-air missiles, not for dogfights, but for eliminating bombers or intruding aircraft before they drop payloads, and are often controlled via ground-based radar guidance, working in tight coordination with air defence control nodes.

In contrast, multirole fighters handle air-to-ground attacks, close air support, and air superiority campaigns. The interceptor, however, is a specialist. A bouncer. A chaser. A shield.

Where do interceptors fit in the kill chain? In modern integrated air defence, once a radar detects an incoming aircraft, the command classifies it and decides on engagement. Missiles may be launched, but if the threat is manned, evasive, or ambiguous, an interceptor is scrambled.

Once airborne, the interceptor uses its onboard radar, infrared sensors, and the pilot's judgment to pursue, identify, and—if needed—eliminate the target. This makes interceptors particularly vital in cases of radar blackouts or jamming, or civilian aircraft gone rogue, or when unknown aircraft violate no-fly zones, and in electronic warfare where IFF IFF (Identification Friend or Foe) systems fail.

India's air defence relies on fighters that double as interceptors. The MiG-21 Bison, once the mainstay, is now phased out. A heavyweight with excellent radar range and air-to-air capability is the Sukhoi Su-30MKI, while the Mirage 2000 scrambled during Balakot retaliation. The Rafale is the IAF's newest and most capable interceptor platform. Future assets include the indigenous Tejas Mk1A, and long-term proposals for AMCA (Advanced Medium Combat Aircraft) will likely carry AD-interceptor profiles.

These aircraft are stationed at air defence alert (ADA) bases around the country, able to launch within minutes—guided initially by radar, then by the pilot's own sight and instinct.

Unlike missiles, which, once launched, are committed, interceptors give air defence flexibility. They can shadow suspicious aircraft, demand identification via radio, change rules of engagement in real time, and abort the mission if needed.

They carry with them human judgment, which, even in the age of AI, remains essential for discerning friend from foe, civilian from combatant, error from attack.

The Rafale Fighter of the Indian Air Force
(Courtesy: PIB)

CHAPTER 9

◆◆◆

Command & Control—The Brain of Air Defence

If radar is the heart, missiles the fists, and interceptors the sword arm, then Command and Control (C2) is the brain—the part that fuses perception and judgment, orchestrates the response, and ensures that every element acts in concert rather than chaos.

Without a coherent C2 architecture, radars may detect but fail to share, missiles may launch but collide with friendly aircraft, interceptors may fly blind or late, and enemy deception may succeed in splitting sectors or overwhelming nodes.

Modern air defence is no longer about individual brilliance but about coordinated efficiency. That coordination happens in C2 centres—networked bunkers, mobile command vans, underground nodes, or airborne AWACS (Airborne Warning And Control System) hubs.

Key Functions of Command and Control in AD

Sensor Fusion: Taking inputs from multiple radars (ground, airborne, naval, space) and integrating them into a single threat picture.

Threat Classification & Prioritisation: Distinguishing decoys from real targets, sorting by speed, altitude, flight path, and intent.

Weapon Assignment: Deciding whether to launch an interceptor, fire a missile, or scramble an aircraft—and which unit should do so.

Airspace Deconfliction: Coordinating Identification Friend or Foe (IFF) responses across services to avoid friendly fire incidents (e.g., the tragic Mi-17 shootdown near Srinagar in 2019), and preventing collisions and overlaps.

Authority Assignment: Deciding when a local battery can auto-fire vs. when HQ must approve.

Civil-Military Coordination: Deconflicting with civilian air traffic, issuing city alerts, and integrating disaster response if required.

Redundancy and Resilience: Surviving jamming, cyber attacks, and kinetic strikes on key nodes through hardened or mobile backup systems.

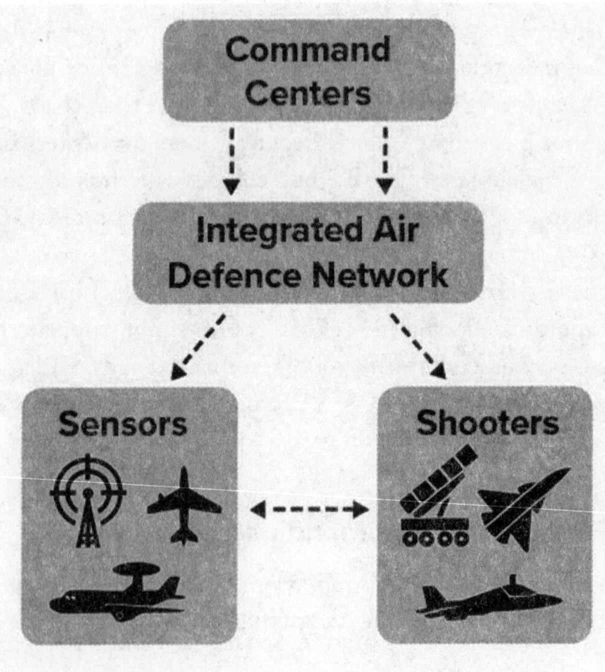

The First Brain: SAGE and the Cold War Dream

In the 1950s, the United States believed the Soviets might launch waves of bombers across the Arctic. Radar could see them coming, but there was no system that could pull all that data together and decide who should respond.

So the U.S. built SAGE—the Semi-Automatic Ground Environment—a massive room-filling computer that connected radar stations across North America to command centres via telephone lines. Operators sat at round cathode-ray screens, using light pens to assign targets and launch aircraft.

It was slow, prone to glitches, and vulnerable to a well-placed wrench. But it was revolutionary.

For the first time in history, a nation could see its skies in real time, coordinate defence decisions, and respond within minutes. It was the first brain of air defence, made of vacuum tubes and optimism.

The Acronyms

The terms C2, C3, and C4 represent progressively complex layers of military command systems.

C2 stands for Command and Control: It refers to the authority and direction exercised by a military commander over assigned forces. It includes decision-making and the systems used to issue orders.

C3 adds Communications to the mix: Command, Control, and Communications. This involves not just deciding and directing, but doing so reliably across secure, integrated channels—especially in the chaos of combat.

C4 includes a fourth element: Computers. So, Command, Control, Communications, and Computers. This recognises the centrality of computational systems, digital networks, data processing, and automation in modern warfare.

Some models even extend to C5ISR or C6, bringing in Intelligence, Surveillance, and Reconnaissance, acknowledging the role of information dominance.

India's C4: The Birth of IACCS

India's IACCS is a prime example of a modern C4 grid. It connects the air force, army AD units, and radar sensors nationwide, provides commanders with a real-time airspace picture, and allows decision nodes to act within seconds—not minutes.

Without this system, even the best radars or missiles would operate in isolation. With it, they become a single living organism, aware, decisive, and increasingly autonomous.

Until the late 1990s, India's air defence was siloed and analog. The air force ran its radar grid. The army manned gun and missile systems. The navy tracked aerial threats at sea. But the systems didn't talk to each other.

Kargil changed that. Though the war was fought at high altitudes with little air threat, the conflict exposed how vulnerable India was to a lack of real-time coordination across services.

So in the 2000s, the Indian Air Force began developing a system that would digitise India's radar network, share data securely between branches, and allow decentralised response with central oversight.

The result was IACCS—a networked command system now operational across India's five operational commands, connected to both static and mobile radars, missile batteries, and aircraft command centres.

◆◆◆

At its best, IACCS can detect an incoming threat from Pakistan or China within seconds, cross-check its path, speed, and signature with known threat libraries, assign an Akash or S-400 battery to intercept, scramble fighters as backup, and alert civil aviation authorities—all within a minute.

This is not science fiction. This is operational reality. During *Operation Sindoor*, it was IACCS that lit up when loitering munitions appeared over Punjab.

India's Integrated Air Command and Control System (IACCS) (Courtesy: PIB)

◆◆◆

In war, one of the first targets is not a missile or aircraft, but the command network, because if the brain is non-functional, the rest of the system also plunges into chaos. Every modern adversary knows this.

In Ukraine, Russian cyber operations and kinetic strikes on AD command posts blinded air defences, creating windows of opportunity for missile strikes.

This is why modern C4 systems like IACCS are:

Redundant: With fallback nodes in mobile vans, hardened bunkers, and even airborne relays.

Encrypted: With frequency-hopping links and quantum-safe protocols.

Layered: So that if one sector is blinded, another can compensate.

The brain must never sleep, never blink, never be in one place alone.

When the Brain Gives a False Alarm: Three Misses

24 November 1961 – Nebraska

At Strategic Air Command (SAC) Headquarters, the corridors buzzed with routine. Alerts were low. The Cold War, while ever-present, was quiet that night. And then the screens went dark.

In one minute, SAC operators could talk to NORAD (North American Aerospace Defense Command). In the next, total silence. Not just one radar station. Not just one command line. But all of them—NORAD, Ballistic Missile Early Warning System (BMEWS) sites in Greenland, Alaska, and the UK, and even backup circuits—went offline. Redundant, hardened, secure systems, went dark together. The odds were infinitesimal.

To SAC officers trained to anticipate the worst, this wasn't a glitch. It was a message: "We are under attack."

No missiles had been sighted, no blips tracked, and no satellites flashed warnings, but the lack of communication was as loud as an explosion.

SAC followed its war plan. Orders were issued. Crews were dispatched. Bomber pilots were scrambled to readiness, nuclear payloads loaded, and engines powered on for immediate takeoff.

In nuclear defence, silence was not passive—it was a signal. A pre-emptive strike could be underway, having targeted communication nodes first. With no incoming radar signature, this could be the stealth before the storm. The clock was ticking. The bombers began to roll.

As the airborne alert force prepared to launch, one final cross-check remained: the aircraft already in the sky—training flights, recon sorties, test missions. They were now the only eyes and ears left.

What they saw changed everything.

Nothing.

No missiles rising on the horizon. No blasts. No infrared signatures. No EMP (Electromagnetic Pulse) flickers. The silence, it turned out, was just silence. Hours later, the truth surfaced.

The blackout had not been caused by Soviet sabotage, EMP warfare, or a first strike. It had been caused by a single faulty relay switch—a component barely larger than a shoebox—in a communication relay station in Colorado. One switch. One link in the chain. And the entire U.S. nuclear command structure had woken on the edge of retaliation.

The system had been engineered with redundancy. But that redundancy was routed through a single point of failure. It wasn't discovered until the moment it mattered most.

23 May 1967 – Morning

At the North American Aerospace Defense Command's (NORAD's) radar stations across the Northern Hemisphere, things suddenly went dark. Among them were three Ballistic Missile Early Warning System (BMEWS) sites—recently upgraded, now inexplicably silent.

In the logic of Cold War defence, such coordinated jamming could mean only one thing: a Soviet first strike was imminent. At Strategic Air Command, nuclear-capable bombers were placed on alert. Fighters were readied. Orders moved up the chain.

Then, just before the strike preparations reached launch threshold, a message came down from NORAD's space weather division: It's not the Soviets—it's the sun.

A massive solar flare and coronal mass ejection had blasted Earth's atmosphere, disrupting high-frequency communications. The radars hadn't been jammed—they'd been blinded by space weather.

The bombers stood down. The war that never happened receded back into silence.

The sun had caused a glitch. But for a moment, it had nearly triggered nuclear night.

9 November 1979 – 3:00 AM, Colorado Springs

Inside the granite fortress of Cheyenne Mountain, home to NORAD, a low hum of routine filled the dark, climate-controlled command centre. Monitors flickered. Technicians hunched over consoles. It was the Cold War's midnight hour, but nothing unusual stirred.

Then, at precisely 3:00 AM, a red light began flashing.

The screen showed something unimaginable: 250 Soviet ballistic missiles had been launched—presumably from Siberia—streaking across space toward targets across the United States. The data was being relayed to Peterson Air Force Base, Strategic Air Command (SAC) HQ at Offutt, the National Military Command Center in the Pentagon, and the Alternate Command Center in Raven Rock.

In a matter of seconds, phones rang like alarm bells. The console room erupted in tightly coiled urgency. The war plan was clear: a retaliatory launch decision had to be made within three to seven minutes.

NORAD did what it had been trained to do. Protocols kicked in. Commands were issued. Systems engaged.

This was the moment everyone had feared since the dawn of the nuclear age: the first strike scenario.

◆◆◆

In Washington, National Security Advisor Zbigniew Brzezinski was awoken in the night by a secure call. The voice was calm but final:

"Sir, we have a confirmed launch. 250 missiles inbound."

He did not wake his wife. If this were real, they would all be gone before she could open her eyes.

Brzezinski was told that the President would need to decide—within six minutes—whether to launch America's entire nuclear arsenal in response. Everything depended on the assumption that what the computers were showing was not a glitch.

Then, a new update.

"Correction: updated count is 2,200 missiles inbound."

The full weight of Armageddon now seemed to be in motion. Bombers were prepped. Missile silos stood by. SAC was locked in.

And yet... the radar screens were oddly quiet.

◆◆◆

Racing against the clock, NORAD switched to PAVE PAWS (PAVE Phased Array Warning System), the U.S. space-based early warning system that monitored real-world ICBM (Intercontinental Ballistic Missile) launches.

Its feeds showed nothing.

No plumes in Siberia. No missile trails. No radar contacts. Nothing at all.

In a moment of staggering relief—and deep confusion—the alert was downgraded. The United States stood down.

No missiles. No war. No judgment day.

Just a phantom apocalypse born from a computer screen.

◆◆◆

Later, investigators discovered the cause: someone at NORAD had accidentally inserted a training tape into a live operational computer. The system had interpreted the simulation as a real attack.

The machines did what they were told. They didn't know it was fake. But the humans didn't know it was fake either.

It was not until multiple independent systems cross-verified the data that it became clear: this was a false alarm, one that could have escalated into the end of civilisation.

Coincidentally, Senator Charles H. Percy of Illinois was visiting NORAD at that exact moment. He witnessed the panic firsthand—generals scrambling, phones lighting up, bombers being readied.

When word reached Capitol Hill, Congress was stunned. A war had almost started, and most of them had slept through it. It was, quite literally, a war game mistaken for war.

In the months following the November event, NORAD experienced three more false alarms: Two caused by faulty computer chips, and one severe enough to force the National Emergency Airborne Command Post to taxi into launch position at Andrews Air Force Base.

The entire nuclear command apparatus had proven shockingly fragile, not just to malice, but to accidents.

◆◆◆

In the Kremlin, news of the false alarm caused panic of a different kind. Soviet leader Leonid Brezhnev sent a rare direct communication to President Jimmy Carter, stating:

"Such a mistake is fraught with tremendous danger. I think you will agree with me that there should be no errors in such matters."

Carter did agree.

The incident led to improvements in redundancy, simulation safeguards, and a renewed emphasis on human-in-the-loop verification.

But the truth lingered, quietly: we had nearly destroyed ourselves over a training file.

◆◆◆

The next evolution of C2 is already underway. AI-assisted battle managers can suggest responses before a human does, and autonomous kill chains act within seconds—but still seek human confirmation. Cross-domain fusion—integrating not just air, but space, cyber, and naval inputs into one battle cloud—makes the air defence system less a chain of parts, and more a thinking web—aware, adaptive, and always listening.

And at the centre of it will always be a brain that never fires a bullet, but ensures every bullet knows where to go.

CHAPTER 10

◆◆◆

Electronic Warfare—The Nervous System of Air Defence

In the theatre of air defence, radar may act as the heart that senses, missiles as fists that strike, interceptors as swords that chase, and command centres as the brain that decides. But without a functioning nervous system, even the strongest body is blind, clumsy, and easily misled.

This nervous system is Electronic Warfare (EW)—an invisible realm of signals and pulses, of waves and deception, where a war is fought not with steel, but with static.

Unlike missiles or interceptors, EW systems don't destroy the enemy. They manipulate perception. And in a world of split-second alerts and kill chains, changing perception can be as lethal as pulling a trigger.

A War Fought in Frequencies

At its core, Electronic Warfare operates across three tasks:

Electronic Support (ESM): Listening in—detecting radar emissions, mapping enemy air defence layouts, identifying threats by their signatures.

Electronic Attack (EA): Disrupting—jamming radars, spoofing IFF signals, blinding fire-control systems, or feeding false inputs.

Electronic Protection (EP): Defending—hardening friendly systems against spoofing, jamming, and deception.

Together, these functions make EW the unseen thread connecting all layers of air defence—from the moment a threat appears on radar to the decision to launch.

The Phantom Strike: Syria, 2007

On 6 September 2007, Israeli jets launched *Operation Orchard*, a surprise airstrike deep inside Syria to destroy a suspected nuclear facility.

What puzzled the world wasn't just the audacity of the mission—it was that Syria never saw the jets coming.

Their sophisticated Russian-built radars never lit up. No fighters scrambled. No SAMs fired. It was as if the skies went blank.

Post-strike analysis suggested that Israel had employed a combination of radar spoofing, communication jamming, and false target projection, possibly using a version of the Suter EW system—penetrating Syrian radar feeds and showing nothing where the jets actually were.

The Syrians weren't caught asleep. They were electronically paralysed.

Ground-Based Sensors

Ground-based sensors are the unsung sentinels of air defence—silent, passive, and crucial. Often overshadowed by the glamour of radar domes and interceptor jets, these low-profile, high-precision instruments form the bedrock of situational awareness, especially in the realm of Electronic Warfare (EW) and non-radar detection.

Ground sensors refer to non-radar, passive or semi-active devices placed strategically across terrain to detect low-flying aircraft, drones, or stealth platforms, track radio frequency (RF) emissions, communications chatter, or radar pulses, and to sense vibrations, heat, sound, or electromagnetic signatures from aerial vehicles.

These include RF direction finders, acoustic arrays, infrared (IR) cameras, seismic sensors (used primarily in base security but increasingly in drone detection), and passive radar receivers, which "listen" to ambient EM waves and detect disturbances caused by moving objects.

They work best in dense terrain, urban zones, or electronic warfare environments where active systems like radars are degraded or denied.

In any air defence scenario where radar is jammed, communications are spoofed, or satellite data is blocked, ground sensors serve as fallback awareness nodes. They operate passively, meaning they do not emit detectable signals—making them immune to anti-radiation attacks. They can locate sources of jamming or triangulate spoofed signals and provide uninterrupted coverage in valleys, forests, or urban sprawl where radars may have blind spots.

During conflicts in Syria and Ukraine, passive sensor grids have been used to identify small drones, loitering munitions, and jammers, often triggering countermeasures before the threat was visually confirmed.

India is gradually integrating ground sensor grids across sensitive borders and high-value areas. The DRDO (Defence Research and Development Organisation) has developed passive coherent location systems and optical detection units for low-RCS (Radar Cross Section) targets.

At frontline bases, multimodal sensor fusion platforms are being tested—where acoustic, thermal, and RF sensors operate together to cue radars or air defence guns.

In Kashmir and along the Western Front, UAV detection networks now often begin with ground-based RF sniffers—systems that can detect even a micro-UAV's control signal from several kilometres away.

Ground sensors aren't just about finding the enemy. They can detect the onset of electronic attack—sudden bursts of jamming or signal fog. They can also map enemy EW activity in real time, helping command centres avoid zones of signal distortion, and can cue precision air defence fire, especially with VSHORAD and point defence systems like L-70 or ZU-23-2.

In future networked warfare, ground sensors will serve as autonomous watchmen, each node contributing to a central, fused threat map. Their stealth and persistence will be crucial in keeping AD systems conscious and reactive, especially under electronic assault.

The future of ground-based sensing in air defence lies in: sensor fusion by combining acoustic, seismic, and RF data into a unified threat picture. AI-assisted pattern recognition will identify drone swarms, jammers, or stealth aircraft from faint anomalies, while distributed autonomous grids will be sensor networks that don't rely on central links and can operate in denied environments.

As the air domain grows more complex, these buried, listening, watching nodes may be the first to know—and the last to fall silent.

Ground Sensors in the Russo-Ukraine War

Ground sensors—though far less publicised than drones or missiles—are being used extensively and strategically in the Ukraine war, especially in electronic warfare (EW), base protection, and low-altitude air defence roles. Their deployment has become a critical, if understated, part of Ukraine's effort to adapt in a contested electromagnetic battlespace where conventional radars and communication systems are often jammed, spoofed, or destroyed.

One of the primary uses of ground sensors in Ukraine has been detecting enemy radio frequency (RF) emissions. These include control signals from Russian UAVs, including Orlan-10s and Lancet loitering munitions, and the jamming emitters and communication repeaters that are being used to suppress Ukrainian command chains.

Ground sensors—especially passive RF sniffers—help Ukrainian EW teams locate these emissions and triangulate their positions for counter-artillery or drone strikes.

This is particularly useful because passive sensors do not emit, making them less susceptible to being targeted by anti-radiation missiles.

Ukraine's defence of cities and front-line positions relies heavily on early detection of small UAVs, which are often too low-flying or small for traditional radar, and swarm-launched or stealth-modified to avoid standard detection.

To counter this, ground acoustic arrays and RF sensors are deployed around bases and supply depots to listen for rotor noise, even amid artillery din, and pick up telemetry links or control signals from first-person-view (FPV) drones.

In the Kherson and Bakhmut sectors, such sensor nets have reportedly triggered anti-drone gun teams and VSHORAD systems before drones could reach target zones.

Ukraine continues to rely on the legacy ZSU-23-4 "Shilka" and Gepard gun systems. In areas where radar is jammed, ground-based sensors serve as targeting cues, especially for last-mile defence around power plants and mobile air defence units protecting HIMARS (High Mobility Artillery Rocket System) and artillery.

Ukrainian units are also reported to be testing sensor fusions, where audio, thermal, and electromagnetic signatures are fused into a basic track, then handed off to a manually operated air defence gun.

Ground sensors, while useful, also face challenges. In muddy, frozen, or rubble-strewn terrain, false positives are common. Sensors themselves can be detected and destroyed by aggressive Russian EW reconnaissance units. Power supply and data transmission remain vulnerabilities.

To adapt, Ukrainian forces often deploy disposable sensor clusters, cheap and unlinked from the main grid, to lure or misdirect enemy jammers and suppressive fire.

In the Ukraine war, ground sensors have not been game-changers—but they have been game-sustainers. In a battlefield flooded with jamming and deception, they serve as resilient points of awareness, giving commanders precious seconds of warning or a whisper of truth when the sky goes silent. They may not headline the war, but they help keep Ukraine's air defence system stitched together at the seams.

India's EW Ecosystem and the "Fence"

India has developed its own EW capabilities in tandem with its air defence grid. The IAF and DRDO have fielded the Sangraha and Himashakti EW systems for aircraft and ground units, while Samyukta is a joint Army–IAF platform for battlefield signal intelligence.

Combat aircraft like the Mirage 2000 and Sukhoi Su-30MKI are equipped with sophisticated jamming pods and radar warning receivers. Upgrades to AD systems include electronic counter-countermeasures (ECCM) to resist spoofing and jamming.

But gaps remain, especially against low-cost swarm drones and commercial UAVs operating below traditional radar thresholds. These threats are often radio-controlled, requiring real-time EW defence to suppress command links or hijack frequencies.

India's electric fence system along the Line of Control (LoC) with Pakistan in Jammu & Kashmir—officially known as the Anti-Infiltration Obstacle System (AIOS)—incorporates sensors. In its more advanced segments, those sensors interface with electronic surveillance and EW assets, forming a tactical-level input into India's broader air defence and electronic warfare grid.

While AIOS was initially a physical barrier (wires, posts, and lights), over the years it has been digitised and sensorised to act as a smart fence, capable of detecting, tracking, and cueing responses to both ground and low-altitude aerial threats, including drones and loitering munitions.

The electric fence consists of multiple tiers of concertina wire, electrified fencing, thermal imagers, night vision cameras, seismic and vibration sensors, passive infrared (PIR) detectors and ground-based radar patches (in select areas).

These are managed by Indian Army and BSF units, particularly in sectors like Kupwara, Uri, Poonch, and Rajouri, where infiltration and drone drops are frequent.

Increasingly, these sensors feed into the EW/AD Grid. Here's how:

Tactical Inputs into Local Air Defence—Sensors along the LoC (Line of Control) detect low-flying drones and radio-controlled UAVs, especially at night. RF sniffers and passive signal interceptors pick up command-and-control frequencies used by drones launched from across the border. These detections are relayed in real-time to battalion-level air defence units and electronic warfare detachments.

Linkage with EW Assets—I high-risk sectors, electronic warfare vehicles and jamming units operate in sync with the smart fence—ready to jam drone links, spoof coordinates, or identify RF anomalies for counter-action Some sensor data from these fences feeds into India's IACCCS (Integrated Air Command and Control System) via local command centres, enabling correlated threat assessments.

Counter-Drone Operations—Along the Jammu sector, where drones are used for weapon drops, AI-powered sensor feeds from the fence are used to trigger interceptor fire, alert Quick Reaction Teams, or launch radio jammersmounted on all-terrain vehicles.

The sensorised fence is not standalone. In active sectors, it serves as an early warning and data generation layer, particularly useful when radar coverage is blocked by mountainous terrain. In the event of jamming or communication blackouts, many fence sectors now have autonomous triggers and alarms, ensuring continuity of surveillance. The smart fence data increasingly cues anti-drone rifle teams and soft-kill systems (like frequency jammers or microwave guns), offering a low-tech but effective layer of air defence from the ground up.

The smart fencing system along the LoC is no longer just a border barrier—it is a tactical layer of India's electronic warfare and air defence ecosystem. In an era of drone incursions and signal spoofing, it serves as both a tripwire and a trigger, allowing India to defend its skies not only from above, but from the soil itself.

Electronic Warfare is subtle. It doesn't explode. It doesn't roar. But its effects can be catastrophic. A radar jammed at the wrong moment; a missile fed the wrong coordinates; a command centre fed noise instead of a signal. And just like that, the system seizes.

Tomorrow's air defence will be shaped not by more radars or bigger missiles, but by smarter electronic reflexes:

AI-enabled spectrum mapping.

Quantum-resistant communications.

Hyperspectral sensors that see past deception.

UAV-based jammers that escort missiles to disrupt AD nodes just before impact.

In this age, to win the war in the sky, one must first win the war over the airwaves.

Electronic Warfare: The Sixth Domain

Electronic Warfare (EW) is much larger than just its role in Air Defence. While air defence remains one of its most dramatic and immediate applications—blinding radars, jamming missile seekers, spoofing drone controls—EW is, in truth, a foundational pillar of modern warfare across land, sea, air, cyber, and space domains.

Think of EW not as a specific system or tactic, but as a domain of warfare in itself, one that spans spectrum dominance, information control, signal disruption, and deception. Its goal is simple: control the electromagnetic environment to your advantage and deny it to the adversary.

In land warfare, EW systems jam enemy radios, cutting off tactical communication between squads or armoured units, disrupt battlefield GPS signals, causing navigation errors or misfires in artillery systems, detect and track mobile command posts by triangulating RF emissions, and trigger or jam remote-controlled IEDs (Improvised Explosive Devices), which are often linked to wireless detonators.

EW at sea is crucial for ship protection against anti-ship missiles, using soft-kill measures like chaff, decoy flares, and radar jammers. Electronic support measures (ESM) help detect enemy radars, sonar buoys, or missile lock-ons. Undersea EW is in the form of acoustic decoys and sonar jamming counters submarines and torpedoes.

Modern warships are essentially floating electronic platforms, with as much emphasis on spectrum dominance as on torpedoes or guns.

While EW and cyber warfare are distinct, they often converge in modern doctrine. EW systems can insert malicious code via over-the-air injections into data links or battlefield networks. Cyber tools can disable EW systems or corrupt the algorithms used in jammers and sensors. Both are used to spread disinformation, delay decisions, and erode trust in systems.

In joint operations, EW assets might jam a UAV's downlink, while cyber assets target the command software that controls the UAV fleet.

In space and strategic warfare, satellites depend on clean, uninterrupted signals for navigation (GPS/GAGAN (GPS Aided GEO Augmented Navigation)), missile warning (SBIRS (Space-Based InfraRed System)/NETRA (NEtwoking TRaffic Analysis)), and ISR (Intelligence, Surveillance, Reconnaissance).

EW can jam satellite uplinks or downlinks, spoof GNSS (Global Navigation Satellite System) signals, making units think they're in the wrong location, and interfere with early warning radars or downlink telemetry.

China, Russia, and the U.S. have all developed space EW systems capable of attacking satellites non-kinetically—through dazzlers, signal noise, or uplink spoofing.

Strategic command and nuclear deterrence is one of the least visible but most chilling EW frontiers. Strategic communication networks (for example, those used to relay nuclear launch orders) are hardened against jamming and spoofing. EW units train to protect and disrupt high-frequency burst communication, especially in the case of a first strike scenario.

False radar returns or spoofed missile signatures could trick early warning systems—potentially pushing nations toward catastrophic decisions.

That's why EW is deeply embedded in nuclear doctrine, not just as a tactical tool but as a strategic stabiliser or destabiliser.

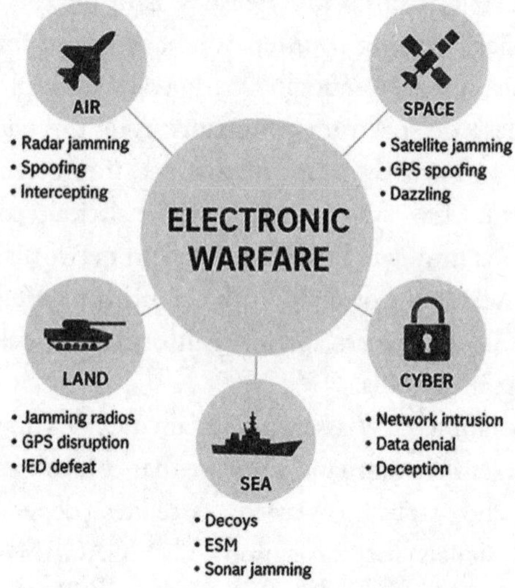

From battlefield skirmishes to orbital standoffs, Electronic Warfare is not a support function. It is a theatre—the sixth theatre. A battlespace. A war unto itself.

In the age of connected sensors, AI-driven kill chains, and network-centric warfare, the one who owns the spectrum owns the fight.

Air defence is just one nerve cluster in this larger nervous system. But the brain, the eyes, and the voice of modern warfare all speak in signals—and Electronic Warfare is the power to interrupt, mimic, or erase that speech.

CHAPTER 11

◆◆◆

Satellites in Air Defence—Eyes in the Orbit

Satellites can indeed be considered a critical extension of the nervous system in air defence—but only partially and contextually within Electronic Warfare (EW). They don't jam or spoof directly, but they enable, enhance, and defend the EW and command architecture by acting as the high-altitude nerves—carrying vision, data, and reflexes across continents.

That said, satellites are too central, too powerful, and too multifaceted in air defence to be folded into EW entirely. They deserve a dedicated exploration of their role as the eyes in the stratosphere.

◆◆◆

When a missile is launched in Central Asia, it takes less than 30 seconds for a satellite in geostationary orbit to see the heat plume. Before any radar picks it up, before any siren sounds, the event is already flagged in orbit—its trajectory plotted, its estimated impact point calculated.

This is not science fiction. It's standard operating procedure.

In the architecture of modern air defence, satellites are the orbital backbone—quiet, continuous, and omnipresent. They act as sensors, seeing what ground-based radars cannot, as messengers, relaying data across hemispheres, as referees, distinguishing friend from foe across blacked-out zones, and increasingly, as targets and protectors in their own right.

During the Cold War, both the U.S. and the Soviet Union developed infrared missile detection satellites—the DSP (Defense Support Program) and Oko, respectively. Their sole job was to scan the horizon for the intense heat signatures of ICBM launches.

These satellites were crucial in narrowing the decision window: if a missile launched, they bought minutes of early warning—precious time for scrambling interceptors or activating nuclear deterrents.

Today, systems like the U.S. SBIRS and India's planned satellite-based BMD (Ballistic Missile Defence) warning layers continue this task with far greater precision and multi-band detection.

◆◆◆

Air defence depends not only on what is seen, but on how fast that information moves.

Satellites provide secure communication relays between radars and command posts, fighters and ground controllers, and missile batteries and higher headquarters.

In rugged terrain—say, the Himalayas—where ground comms fail, satellites ensure that no part of the kill chain goes dark. India's GSAT (Geosynchronous SATellite) series and proposed GSAT-7C for defence forces are meant to enable encrypted battlefield connectivity, making even mobile AD units a part of the real-time grid.

Without this, a sensor might detect—but the shooter would never know.

◆◆◆

Satellites also provide the terrain layer of air defence—through high-resolution imaging satellites like India's Cartosat (Cartography Satellite) and RISAT (Radar Imaging SATellite) series. SAR (Synthetic Aperture Radar) satellites that see through clouds and darkness. Orbital reconnaissance helps identify enemy radar setups, missile silos, or mobile AD vehicles across borders.

This data feeds into target libraries, mission planning software, and weapon guidance systems. Every air defence strike—kinetic or electronic—begins with an orbital snapshot.

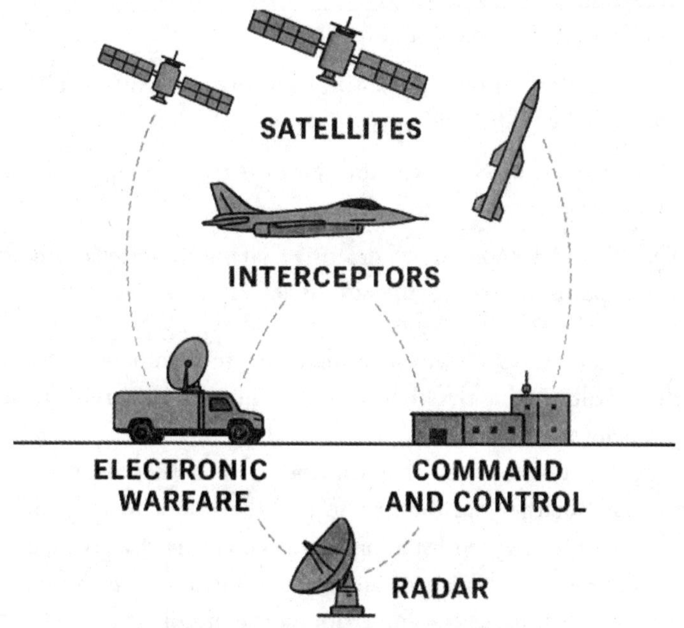

SATELLITES IN AIR DEFENCE

The New Battlespace: ASAT and Satellite Jamming

But space is not passive.

In 2007, China destroyed one of its own satellites using a ground-launched missile. In 2019, India followed with Mission Shakti, shooting down a satellite to demonstrate anti-satellite (ASAT) capability.

Why? Because in modern war, taking out the enemy's eyes is as valuable as shooting down their aircraft.

Satellites can now be jammed to disrupt communication, spoofed to mislead GPS-guided weapons, blinded by lasers, and even hacked to feed false telemetry or shut down AD links.

This has led to the rise of space-based electronic protection measures and hardened satellite protocols—a digital armour in orbit.

India's air defence grid is evolving with satellites at its core:

Integration of GAGAN (GPS Aided GEO Augmented Navigation) for precision targeting.

Use of Defence Image Processing and Analysis Centres (DIPAC) for orbital data fusion.

Proposed use of Netra satellites for near-real-time space domain awareness.

Ongoing development of defensive satellite constellations that can support air defence operations across two active fronts.

As India moves toward a unified theatre command structure, satellites will become the high command in orbit, supervising every action below.

Satellites do not fire. They do not scream. They do not chase intruders. But they are the first to see, the fastest to inform, and often, the only ones left listening when everything else goes dark.

In the nervous system of air defence, satellites are the highest nerves, connecting every fingertip to the mind, every reflex to reason. They are not just tools. They are the perspective from which the whole war is mapped.

CHAPTER 12

◆◆◆

AWACS and AEW&C in Air Defence—Ears in the Stratosphere

Complementing the satellites in the sky are the Airborne Warning and Control System (AWACS) and its lighter cousin, AEW&C (Airborne Early Warning and Control)—the crows' nests of the sky—moving sentinels that watch and hear farther, higher, and with greater nuance than anything anchored to earth.

The idea of airborne radar didn't emerge in a lab. It came from necessity, and from a war where the ground was too slow and the horizon too short.

From Convoys to Combat Zones

The concept of airborne early warning was born in World War II, when German U-boats began decimating Allied shipping in the Atlantic. Britain's Royal Air Force experimented with radar-equipped aircraft to spot submarines before they could strike. These were crude setups—bulky sets jammed into bombers—but they worked. The concept had taken flight.

It was the United States, however, that truly operationalised the airborne radar platform. By the 1950s, with Cold War paranoia ascending, the U.S. developed airborne warning aircraft to detect Soviet bombers before they reached American soil. The most famous outcome of that period was the E-3 Sentry, developed by Boeing in the 1970s. With its distinctive rotating radar dome perched like a flying saucer on its back, the E-3 became the visual icon of strategic surveillance—a flying guardian that could see hundreds of kilometres in every direction.

The Role in Air Defence

AWACS changed the very geometry of air defence. Ground-based radar, no matter how powerful, is always limited by the curvature of the Earth. It can see far, but not soon enough. AWACS, flying at high altitudes, overcomes this. They extend the radar horizon, detect low-flying aircraft skimming under radar coverage, and track multiple airborne targets simultaneously across vast stretches of sky.

But their value isn't just in what they see. It's in what they enable.

AWACS aircraft are essentially flying command centres. They direct interceptors toward threats, assign SAM batteries to engage specific targets, and manage complex, multi-axis battles in the air. In the high-speed choreography of modern aerial warfare, where missiles can travel faster than sound and drones can swarm in from dozens of vectors, AWACS give air defence what it needs most—time and structure.

AEW&C: Agile and Tactical

While AWACS platforms are heavy, strategic assets—expensive, complex, and limited in number—AEW&C aircraft are their tactical cousins. Smaller, more agile, and often based on regional jet or turboprop platforms, AEW&Cs are perfect for border surveillance, forward command, and rapid-response scenarios. They may not carry the same radar range, but they can be deployed quickly, operate from smaller airfields, and are harder for adversaries to target.

India's Netra AEW&C system, mounted on a Brazilian Embraer-145 platform, is a prime example. Developed by DRDO,

Netra plays a crucial role in India's border management and localised air defence coordination, especially during high-alert situations like Balakot, Doklam, and *Operation Sindoor*.

Indian Air Force's Netra (Courtesy: PIB)

High Altitude, High Stakes

AWACS and AEW&C platforms are now central to every major air defence strategy. NATO uses them to guard its eastern flank. The U.S. operates them globally from Japan to Qatar. Russia fields the A-50 Mainstay, and China has developed multiple variants of AEW&C based on the Shaanxi Y-8 and KJ-series aircraft.

India, meanwhile, operates a hybrid fleet—three Israeli Phalcon AWACS mounted on Russian IL-76 heavy transports, along with indigenous AEW&Cs. Plans are underway for more powerful indigenous platforms based on Airbus or Boeing airframes, which will give India autonomous, layered airborne control from Leh to Lakshadweep.

The next generation of AEW&C won't just look down at aircraft. They'll scan for hypersonic glide vehicles, track low-orbit satellites, monitor swarm drones, and coordinate automated intercepts using AI-linked fire control systems. Some will be unmanned, flying higher and longer than their crewed counterparts. Others may be deployed in near space, serving as persistent surveillance hubs just below the edge of the atmosphere.

And as future air defence becomes multi-domain—spanning cyber, space, and spectral warfare—these flying platforms will not just relay data. They will interpret it, prioritise it, and act upon it in real time.

But perhaps the most vital role AWACS and AEW&C platforms play is psychological. They are visible. They are audible. When one takes off in a crisis, adversaries notice. When it orbits for hours, it sends a message: we are watching. In moments of tension, these aircraft are flying deterrents, as much political as they are military.

◆◆◆

AWACS and AEW&C platforms are not just eyes and ears in the sky. They are conductors of aerial symphonies, synchronising missiles, fighters, radars, and decisions into a coherent defence posture. Without them, the shield is reactive. With them, it is anticipatory.

And in the wars to come—when threats arrive faster, lower, smaller, and stranger—those aircraft circling high above may be the reason we ever know what's coming at all.

CHAPTER 13

◆◆◆

The Drone War—Crafting a Counter-UAS Doctrine

The threat just got cheaper.

For decades, air defence focused on high-speed, high-altitude threats—fighter jets, cruise missiles, and ballistic rockets. But the 21st century has introduced a new adversary: small, slow, cheap, and intelligent.

The drone—or Unmanned Aerial Systems (UAS) as they are known in military parlance.

Often no larger than a bird, drones can carry high-definition cameras, drop grenades or IEDs, jam communications, deliver contraband or explosives, and act as decoys or data relays

They come in many forms—military-grade MALE (Medium-Altitude Long-Endurance) UAVs, kamikaze drones, FPV (First Person View) loitering munitions, and commercial quadcopters bought off the shelf. And they come in swarms.

In Jammu, Israel, Syria, Libya, Armenia, and most of all, Ukraine, the drone is no longer a reconnaissance novelty. It is a mainstream weapon. Existing air defence systems are too slow, too expensive, or too blind to stop them all.

This is where Counter-UAS (C-UAS) doctrine steps in.

◆◆◆

The threat posed by drones is different from that of conventional air targets. They are:

Low-altitude (often below radar horizons)

Low-RCS (radar cross-section, making detection hard)

Highly manoeuvrable

Dispersed and cheap (some cost less than ₹50,000)

In the Ukraine war, for instance, a ₹20,000 FPV drone with an improvised warhead has destroyed tanks worth crores.

In 2021, two drones dropped IEDs on an Indian Air Force station in Jammu—a first-of-its-kind attack on a military base inside Indian territory. No radar saw them. No missile was launched. They simply arrived.

Elements of a Counter-UAS Doctrine

To counter these threats, the C-UAS doctrine has three main pillars:

Detection

Passive RF Sensors: Detect control signals or telemetry links.

Electro-Optical/Infrared Cameras (EO/IR): Used for visual and thermal tracking.

Acoustic Arrays: Pick up the high-pitched rotor hum of small drones.

Low-altitude Radar: Modified to track slow, low-flying targets.

In India, DRDO's Bharat Drone Detection System uses a mix of EO/IR, radar, and RF analysis to triangulate positions and classify threats.

Decision

C-UAS doctrine requires:

Rapid classification (friendly, civilian, hostile)

Target validation (armed? reconnaissance?)

Rules of Engagement (RoE) clarity: Can a drone over a civilian site be shot down?

This step must be automated but human-supervised, especially in urban or peacetime settings.

Neutralisation (The Kill)

Options are broadly split into:

Soft Kill

RF jamming (blocks communication)

GNSS spoofing (misleads navigation)

Protocol manipulation (hijacks control)

Hard Kill

Nets (projectile or aerial)

Directed Energy Weapons (lasers or microwave guns)

Guns (manual or radar-cued)

Missiles (only in military scenarios)

India is testing systems like D-4 Drone Shield, Smash-2000 rifles, and swarm-neutralising jammers in border areas.

India's Challenges and Adaptations

India's current radar grid is not optimised for very low-altitude threats in border areas, especially in Punjab, Jammu, and the Northeast.

Border bases have started installing perimeter jammers and 360° EO surveillance. Indian Railways and oil infrastructure are being mapped for drone vulnerability. Airports are also conducting anti-drone rehearsals, integrating ATC with C-UAS teams.

There is no unified RoE yet for drones over Indian cities. Civil Aviation rules restrict drone use, but real-time shootdown protocols—especially for rogue drones over VVIP events—are still maturing.

Drone Swarms and Autonomy

Future C-UAS doctrine must deal with drone swarms, where a dozen or more act in tandem, autonomous drones, with no RF signature to jam, and drone-on-drone combat, using interceptor UAVs. AI-based threat prioritisation and distinguishing toys from threats will be crucial, too.

With drones coordinated in hundreds, air attacks are no longer about overwhelming firepower alone but about cognitive overload, pattern disruption, and algorithmic unpredictability. A swarm is not merely a crowd. It is a networked intelligence in motion, where each drone shares information, reacts to defences, changes trajectory mid-flight, and adapts to losses without command interruption.

The result? An airborne hive mind capable of saturating, confusing, and even defeating sophisticated air defence systems.

The first glimmers came from conflict zones like

Libya, where Turkish-made drones overwhelmed Russian-made Pantsir systems, from Nagorno-Karabakh, where Azerbaijan used Israeli loitering drones and mini-swarms to neutralise Armenian tanks and AD radar, and from Ukraine, where swarms of DIY (Do It Yourself) drones and NATO-supplied UAVs have become a daily part of the sky

These weren't billion-dollar jets. They were often under $1,000 machines equipped with thermal cameras, grenades, or jamming pods—but deployed in numbers and with coordination that completely bypassed traditional SAM logic.

Drone swarms fly low, often below radar coverage, come in large, cheap numbers, use non-ballistic, erratic paths, and can mimic birds, civilian signals, or even go silent.

By the time a missile locks on to a drone, there may be dozens of others on its flank. Fire one missile, and you've overspent to kill a fraction of a swarm. Try to jam them, and the swarm may route itself through a new signal channel.

Swarm logic isn't just fast. It's nonlinear.

To counter swarms, militaries are now racing to develop Directed Energy Weapons (DEWs)—lasers and microwaves that can down multiple drones simultaneously, along with AI-enabled fire control that can track and prioritise swarm members dynamically. Hard-soft kill combinations like jammers, nets, and EMP rounds, followed by kinetic interceptors and counter-drone drones—interceptor UAVs equipped with nets, small arms, or kamikaze logic are also being developed.

What makes drone swarms revolutionary isn't just the tech—it's the economic asymmetry. One BrahMos costs ₹30 crore. A swarm of 100 modified quadcopters might cost ₹10 lakh in total.

If even 10% of that swarm reaches an airbase, radar node, or S-400 battery, the damage is exponential.

Most importantly, the enemy may not be a state, but a well-funded, well-networked non-state actor with a laptop and a lab.

Indian Context

India is adapting fast. Initiatives include Defence AI Council-backed swarm R&D (Research and Development), military exercises in Rajasthan simulating drone swarm strikes on tank convoys and ammo depots, and partnerships with startups for autonomous anti-drone fencing and AI jammers.

But challenges remain. Integration with IACCS is ongoing, while rules of engagement in civilian zones are still murky. Attribution of attacks—particularly from across borders—is complex.

Swarms are no longer science fiction. They are formations already appearing in India's hostile skies—from Jammu to Arunachal.

◆◆◆

In the future, every critical installation will need a layered detection system, a fusion engine for alerts, a menu of countermeasures, and trained personnel ready to act within seconds.

The drone threat is here to stay. And C-UAS is not just a toolkit—it is a culture. Because in the next war, the first intruder may not be a MiG or a missile.

It may be a buzzing quadcopter the size of a crow, carrying a hand grenade, flying just below the radar—and well above the policy.

CHAPTER 14

◆◆◆

Tactical Air Defence—Brigades and Battalions

Tactical Air Defence (TAD)—the down-in-the-mud, front-line face of air defence happens at the brigade and battalion level. You can protect a capital from missiles. But what about a convoy in the open, a bridgehead, or a battalion crossing a river? That's where Tactical Air Defence comes in.

For all the complexity of command centres and long-range radars, wars are ultimately fought where soldiers march, tanks roll, and convoys move under hostile skies. These are not static zones or fortified bases. They are fluid, vulnerable, and exposed—and they demand a different kind of air defence.

TAD is not about defending airspace for hours. It's about surviving it for minutes. It is fast, mobile, and reactive, designed to protect fighting formations—armoured columns, infantry brigades, forward observation posts, logistics hubs, and bridging operations—from air attacks that arrive suddenly and leave destruction in seconds.

How TAD Is Different from Strategic AD

Strategic Air Defence is built for protecting wide zones (cities, airbases, nuclear sites) using large, long-range missile systems (S-400, Patriot) operating from hardened positions with layered radar.

Tactical Air Defence is built for protecting troops on the move using short-range, portable, or vehicle-mounted weapons operating with local sensors and limited warning time, and engaging low-flying, fast-attack threats like helicopters, drones, and strike aircraft.

In short, TAD is the last umbrella over the soldier's head—when everything else is too far, too late, or too big to help.

What TAD Looks Like on the Ground

TAD operates in tiers:

Man-Portable Air Defence Systems (MANPADS)

Examples: Igla, Stinger, RBS 70, and India's upcoming VSHORADS

Carried by a two-man team

Infrared-guided, fire-and-forget missiles

Effective range: ~5–6 kilometres

During the Kargil War, MANPADS units protected Indian artillery from Pakistani helicopter incursions at high altitudes.

Self-Propelled Air Defence Guns

Examples: ZSU-23-4 Shilka, Gepard, L-70 with radar upgrades

Mounted on tracked or wheeled platforms

Effective against low-altitude jets, helicopters, and drones

Short-Range Air Defence Missiles (SHORAD)

Examples: Akash (for semi-mobile), SPYDER SR, Quick Reaction SAMs (QRSAM)

Mounted on trucks or tanks

Radar-guided, integrated with local sensors

These systems protect convoys, bridges, and mobile

headquarters—especially during large-scale manoeuvres.

The Indian Context: Corps-Level TAD

India's air defence at the tactical level is primarily handled by the Corps of Army Air Defence (AAD), operating in tandem with IAF mobile radar detachments.

AAD batteries are embedded with Corps HQs and forward brigades during wartime mobilisation. In sectors like Ladakh, Arunachal, and the Western Desert, these units deploy electro-optical sensors, mobile radar trucks, MANPADS teams, and gun-missile hybrids.

The integration is tight and real-time—every motorised battalion is now a potential target for swarm drones, attack helicopters, or standoff PGMs (Precision Guided Munitions). TAD ensures it doesn't become a helpless target.

TAD in Modern Combat: Lessons from Ukraine

Ukraine has become a textbook case of TAD in action.

Stinger and Igla missiles devastated Russian helicopter assaults early in the war. Mobile SHORAD teams hide in the woods, launch, and relocate before counterstrikes. Drone-spotting platoons, using tablets and thermal imagers, now work directly with anti-air gunners to bring down loitering munitions.

The lesson: small, mobile, and smart beats slow, bulky, and expensive, especially against low-cost, high-volume air threats.

◆◆◆

India and other nations are now expanding their TAD capabilities to handle mini and micro drones (sub-2 kg platforms), loitering munitions, GPS-denied environments, and simultaneous air and artillery saturation attacks.

◆◆◆

The way forward includes AI-based fire control systems that can auto-cue guns, truck-mounted laser weapons for drone swarms, networked MANPADS launchers guided by shared radar feeds, and TAD units tied into the IACCS net to receive faster alerts.

In future battlefields, every infantry battalion will need its own "AD bubble"—fast, self-sufficient, and smart enough to protect the boots on the ground.

Air supremacy no longer means full safety. It means partial denial, because even the smallest enemy drone or chopper can turn a clean advance into a disaster.

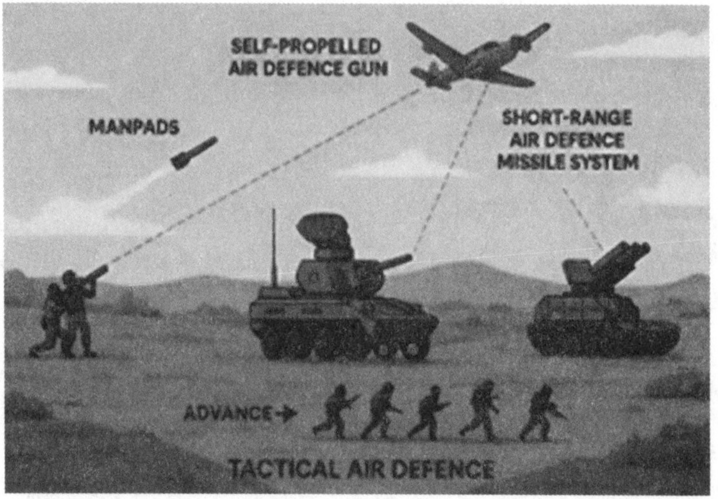

Tactical Air Defence is what keeps the battlefield alive—not with billion-dollar systems, but with tactical reflexes, smart doctrine, and lethal small units.

It doesn't guard capitals.

It guards the war.

CHAPTER 15

◆◆◆

Sea Shields—Naval Air Defence

Unlike land forces, which benefit from terrain, infrastructure, and radar coverage, a ship is an exposed island of steel, silhouetted against the sea, surrounded by nothing, and visible to everything.

At sea, the sky is infinite, but the margin for error is not. Whether it's a fighter jet, a cruise missile, a loitering drone, or a stealthy UAV launched from over the horizon, the clock for a naval crew to react is measured in seconds.

That's why modern naval air defence is no longer just a support function—it is the spinal cord of naval survival.

Pearl Harbor

Pearl Harbor is one of the most pivotal air attacks in naval history, and while it's often remembered as a story of surprise and devastation, it is also a cautionary tale in naval air defence failure, both in terms of readiness and doctrine.

On the morning of 7 December 1941, Japanese aircraft launched a surprise assault on Pearl Harbor, crippling much of the U.S. Pacific Fleet.

At first glance, it may seem like a failure of naval intelligence, not air defence. But deeper analysis reveals that this was, in part, a catastrophic failure of naval air defence doctrine, particularly in three areas.

First, while the radar was operational, it was dismissed. Just before the attack, a mobile SCR-270 radar unit detected an inbound formation of aircraft. The signal was reported. But it was dismissed as a group of B-17 bombers arriving from the mainland. There was no standing alert mechanism to escalate the detection in real-time.

Second, the guns were manned but not ready. Most of the fleet's anti-aircraft guns were unloaded, with ammunition locked in magazines due to peacetime protocol. Only a few gunners were on alert. Those who scrambled to their posts during the attack shot back—but too late, and too few.

Third, there was no layered defence. At the time, the U.S. Navy had not yet developed a multi-tiered AD system. There were no interceptor aircraft on patrol, no integrated radar-fighter communication system, and certainly no missile-based defence. Ships relied solely on guns.

More than 2,400 Americans died. Eight battleships were damaged or sunk. It was the most devastating naval air attack in U.S. history. But from that failure came a revolution.

The U.S. rapidly developed airborne early warning aircraft. Radar-fighter integration led to combat information centres aboard ships. And over time, naval doctrine shifted from gun-only AD to multi-layered missile and sensor-based shields.

In a tragic way, Pearl Harbor birthed modern naval air defence, not in its triumph, but in its absence.

The Threats Above Water

In naval warfare, airborne threats come in many forms—enemy aircraft on strike missions, ship-launched cruise missiles like Harpoon, Exocet, or China's YJ-series, ballistic missiles designed to target carrier groups (e.g., DF-21D), unmanned aerial vehicles (UAVs) used for both surveillance and attack, and swarm drones that can overload even layered defences.

Add to this the challenges of electronic jamming, low-flying sea-skimming missiles, and pop-up attacks from aircraft flying below the radar horizon, and the job of naval air defence becomes a chess game played on a 3D, shifting board.

The Structure of Naval Air Defence

Modern naval air defence follows a layered approach, combining:

Long-Range Detection and Early Warning

Ship-based AESA radars (like MF-STAR on India's destroyers)

Airborne Early Warning (AEW) platforms like the Ka-31 helicopter

In future: drone-based radar pickets and satellite feeds

Outer Layer Interceptors

Medium-to-long-range surface-to-air missiles (SAMs) like Barak-8

Fired at incoming targets 70–100 kilometres away

Often use active radar homing and mid-course correction

Inner Layer/Point Defence

Close-In Weapon Systems (CIWS) like the AK-630, Phalanx, or laser-based CIWS (under development)

React in seconds; last line of defence

Also include short-range SAMs, flares, and decoys

Electronic Warfare and Soft Kill Measures

Radar jamming

Chaff (metallic strips that confuse radar)

Infrared decoys

Directional infrared countermeasures (DIRCM)

This multi-layered shield must operate autonomously, redundantly, and instantly, especially during saturation attacks.

The Indian Navy's Air Defence Doctrine

The Indian Navy has long recognised that air dominance at sea is key to protecting its carrier battle groups (CBGs), destroyer and frigate formations, coastal and island outposts, and shipping lanes and choke points (e.g., Malacca, Hormuz).

Its air defence arsenal includes:

Barak-1 and Barak-8 SAMs

Barak-1: Short-range (~10 kilometres), point defence

Barak-8 (LR-SAM): Developed with Israel; range up to 100 kilometres

Deployed on Kolkata and Vishakhapatnam-class destroyers and Shivalik-class frigates

MF-STAR Radar System

Capable of tracking dozens of targets simultaneously

Provides 360° awareness, guiding SAMs via uplinks

Akash-NG and VL-SRSAM (in development)

Future integration for point defence on smaller corvettes or amphibious platforms

Naval AEW Platforms

Kamov Ka-31 helicopters provide 360° radar coverage

Mounted on the INS Vikrant and other fleet support ships

Future Aspirations

Directed energy weapons for drone swarms

Integrated air and missile defence across ships via data links

Deploying UAVs and UAV swarms as floating radar pickets

Carrier Battle Group (CBG): The Floating AD Grid

A CBG is not just one ship—it's a floating fortress. The carrier (INS Vikramaditya or Vikrant) would likely be accompanied by 2–3

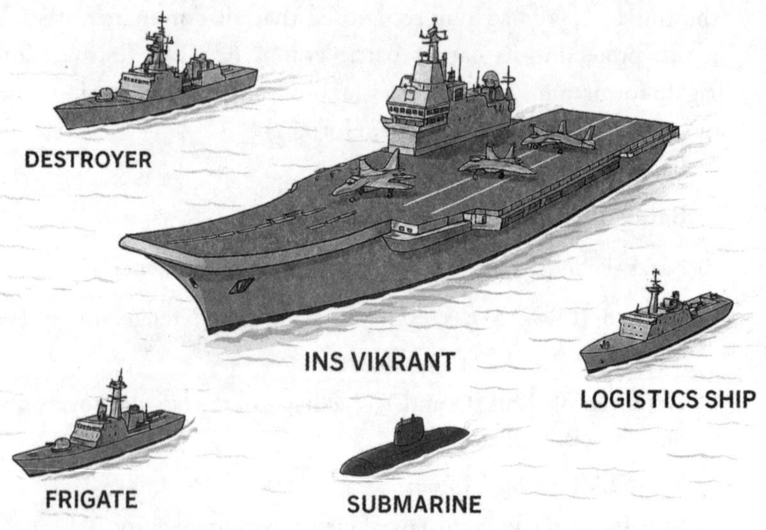

A Carrier Battle Group

destroyers (Barak-8 shield), 1–2 frigates (multi-mission), a logistics ship, and a submarine escort.

Their air defence is networked and overlapping, meaning a target seen by one radar can be engaged by another ship's missile. The carrier itself is rarely the first to fire; it is protected by its escorts. In saturation scenarios, CIWS and SAMs coordinate via combat management systems (CMS).

This doctrine mirrors U.S. CBG tactics—prioritising defence in depth, not brute interception.

Coastal Air Defence and Naval Aviation

Naval air defence isn't just at sea. The coastal command is now protected by optronic and radar towers at strategic locations (Karwar, Port Blair, Vishakhapatnam), Akash and SPYDER systems deployed near naval bases, and naval aviation patrols that track airborne and surface threats before they approach.

India's future plan includes: using space-based maritime domain awareness (MDA), and tying into IAF's IACCS network, ensuring joint control of coastal skies.

◆◆◆

In 2020, during *Operation Samudra Setu*, the Navy evacuated thousands of Indians during the COVID (Coronavirus Disease) pandemic. Though not a wartime operation, destroyers and frigates sailed with Barak missiles armed, radars in combat mode, and CIWS live. Why? Because in contested waters, a single drone, pirate aircraft, or mistaken missile can escalate instantly.

Earlier, in 2006 and 2012, Barak systems successfully intercepted incoming sea-skimming targets during live-fire exercises, validating the "shoot-look-shoot" doctrine.

Operation Trident, executed during the Indo-Pak War in 1971, is remembered as a sea-surface success—with missile boats attacking Karachi harbour—it is what didn't happen overhead that underlines the quiet presence of air defence. During the attack, Indian missile boats like INS Nipat, Nirghat, and Veer were operating dangerously close to the Pakistani coast—within reach of PAF (Pakistan Air Force) jets from Masroor and Faisal air bases. Yet none were intercepted because of a clever trick: the Indian Navy planned the strike for a moonless night, moved fast, and launched before the enemy could react. While the missile boats themselves had no active air defence systems, the fleet had coordinated with the IAF to jam enemy radar and maintained strict radio silence. It was, in essence, a successful air defence-by-stealth—a lesson in how defence is not always about interceptors, but also about denial, deception, and timing.

Challenges and the Way Ahead

Current naval air defence systems are not optimised for coordinated, low-cost swarms or hypersonic missiles (like China's DF-17) that may outpace detection-to-response cycles.

Spectrum congestion and EW vulnerability are important as naval AD systems must operate in heavily jammed environments, and there is a need for AI-based radar filtering and real-time spectrum management.

Also needed is indigenisation and joint command, and the faster rollout of the Akash-NG naval variant. Integration with the Joint Maritime Theatre Command for airspace deconfliction and shared radar pictures can radically improve outcomes.

◆◆◆

At sea, where threats come fast and low, air defence is not a luxury. It is the breathing room for every mission—evacuation, strike, deterrence, or diplomacy.

CHAPTER 16

◆◆◆

Air Defence and the Nuclear Threat

To protect against a nuclear missile is to protect against the end. And that responsibility is shared by many, but guaranteed by none.

Nuclear weapons are not ordinary tools of war. They are strategic instruments—meant not to be used, but to ensure deterrence. In almost every nuclear-armed nation, these weapons are controlled by dedicated strategic commands, with the authority to use them tightly held by political leadership.

But defence against nuclear attack—especially missile-borne—is a different beast. It exists in the overlap between:

> Strategic deterrence (ensuring the threat is never carried out)
> And operational air defence (trying to stop it if it is)

And in that narrow, terrifying space lies the world of missile defence.

The U.S. Example: Layered and Hierarchical

In the United States, nuclear weapons are controlled by the United

States Strategic Command (USSTRATCOM). But defence against nuclear strikes is managed by:

North American Aerospace Defense Command (NORAD) – detection and early warning

Missile Defense Agency (MDA) – development of interceptors like Ground-Based Midcourse Defense (GMD) and THAAD

Northern Command (USNORTHCOM) – execution of continental defence

These systems create a layered architecture, where space-based infrared sensors detect launches, radars (like Sea-Based X-band and Cobra Dane) track them, and ground-based interceptors attempt mid-course kills. If that fails, THAAD or Aegis intercept in the terminal phase.

Importantly, all this is managed separately from nuclear launch authorities. The shield is dispersed—even as the sword remains centralised.

Russia: Doctrine of Integration and Saturation

Russia's nuclear and missile defence structure is more integrated. The Russian Strategic Rocket Forces control ICBMs, while Aerospace Forces (VKS) and Air Defence Troops control defence.

Key elements include the A-135 and A-235 systems, defending Moscow with high-speed interceptors (some nuclear-tipped, a legacy of Cold War logic), and the S-400 and S-500 systems, capable of intercepting medium-range ballistic missiles.

The emphasis is on deception, EW, and redundancy—the doctrine assumes some missiles will penetrate, so it mixes hard kill with passive protection (e.g., bunkers, mobile command posts)

Russia also maintains a "Dead Hand" system (Perimeter), designed to retaliate automatically if command nodes are destroyed, reflecting deep scepticism about interception success.

China: Developing Deterrence, Not Assurance

China's approach has historically been "minimum deterrence"—fewer warheads, less visible posture. But recent years have seen the expansion of silo fields, development of dual-use missile systems, and the increasing interest in missile defence, especially via HQ-19 and HQ-29 systems, akin to THAAD and PAC-3.

China's AD systems are believed to focus more on theatre-level nuclear threats (e.g., from India or U.S. carrier groups) than on full ICBM interception.

India's Case: A Split Between Deterrence and Defence

India's nuclear doctrine is built around No First Use (NFU) and credible minimum deterrence. Nuclear weapons are under the control of the Strategic Forces Command (SFC), reporting directly to the Nuclear Command Authority (NCA) headed by the Prime Minister.

But defence against nuclear weapons involves the Ballistic Missile Defence (BMD) programme, developed by DRDO:

Phase 1: Intercept short-and-medium-range missiles (~2,000 kilometres)

Phase 2: Intercept long-range missiles (ICBM-class)

Swordfish LRTR (Long Range Tracking Radar) and AD-1/AD-2 interceptors, tested for exo- and endo-atmospheric kills

S-400 systems, deployed in strategic locations, offer terminal-phase interception of some ballistic threats

Importantly, India's BMD is still under phased deployment, with no official public declaration of full operational status.

Moreover, civilian protection and missile alert infrastructure—shelters, warning apps, civil drills—are limited, reflecting India's focus on deterrence over interception.

The Ethical and Strategic Tension

Missile defence against nuclear threats presents a paradox. Too strong a shield may undermine deterrence, provoking arms races. Too weak a shield leaves civilians exposed, inviting coercion.

This is why even the best BMD systems (like the U.S. GMD) are limited in number and purpose—designed to intercept limited attacks, not full-scale nuclear exchanges.

India faces similar decisions.

Should BMD be deployed only to protect political/military centres, or expanded to cover population zones?

If a system like S-400 is used to intercept a nuclear-armed missile, who decides if it was successful, and what comes next?

Can accidental or unauthorised launches be intercepted without triggering retaliation?

These are questions that lie at the seam between strategic and tactical, between political judgment and automated systems.

A War Never Fought, But Always Feared

Air defence against nuclear threats is not just about technology. It's about the psychology of leadership, the precision of protocol, and the risk calculus of nations.

A nuclear missile is launched once in fury.

But thousands of minds rehearse its possibility every day.

And when that day comes—if it ever comes—it won't be the missile alone that determines the future.

It will be the readiness of the shield, the clarity of the doctrine, and the judgment of the men and women who must decide in seconds, what the sky means, and whether it can be saved.

CHAPTER 17

◆◆◆

Space Weapons and the Future of Air Defence

Air defence ends at the ceiling of the atmosphere. But space? Space has no ceiling.

For over a century, air defence systems were built with one assumption: that the battlefield ends at the edge of the sky. Missiles, radars, interceptors—all operated within the troposphere and lower stratosphere, chasing aircraft, drones, and incoming warheads.

But that ceiling has cracked. And what lies beyond is not empty space—but contested space.

◆◆◆

Satellites can now blind ground radars, jam air defence frequencies, or feed targeting data to long-range missiles. Enemy weapons can be launched from low Earth orbit. Lasers in space can damage sensors without impact. Kinetic kill vehicles can strike from above with speeds no interceptor can match.

The sky is no longer a roof. It's a window. And through that window, a new class of weapons is beginning to peer downward.

From Guardians to Gladiators

Satellites were once passive eyes and ears of nations. But in the last two decades, the doctrine has shifted. Now, satellites are potential launch platforms, weapons, and targets.

Space weapons fall broadly into three categories:

Kinetic Kill Systems (ASAT): These are physical interceptors launched from Earth to destroy enemy satellites. The 2007 Chinese ASAT test and India's Mission Shakti in 2019 proved this capability. But imagine reversing the equation: what if a space-based system targeted assets on Earth?

Concepts like "rods from God"—tungsten rods dropped from orbit at hypersonic speeds—could act as orbital precision bombs, unstoppable by traditional air defences.

Directed Energy Weapons: Laser systems mounted on satellites could blind missile seekers, disable radar domes, or burn sensor arrays on aircraft, without physical contact. These weapons are silent, invisible, and leave little forensic trace.

Electronic Warfare Satellites: Some satellites are now equipped to jam radar frequencies, intercept encrypted data, or spoof GPS signals. The impact on air defence? Entire command-and-control chains could be deafened before the first missile is fired.

The Threat from Above: How AD Is Vulnerable

Most air defence systems today are designed to detect threats entering from an arc of 0 to 90 degrees relative to the horizon, while launch interceptors are based on ballistic or aerodynamic profiles and use ground-based radar and satellite input for tracking.

But space weapons change everything. A weapon in orbit can attack from directly overhead, bypassing radar arcs. The speed of descent means interceptors may not have time to react while space-based jamming can cut off radar feeds or missile guidance uplinks. Satellites feeding data to long-range missiles make enemy strikes far more precise, even in cluttered airspace.

Traditional AD systems are now part of a larger ecosystem of vulnerability.

The Doctrinal Dilemma

The presence of space weapons forces militaries to ask:

Who controls the uppermost domain?

At what point does a threat from space become a matter of air defence?

Is an attack from orbit considered a strategic strike or a tactical one?

Countries are now developing counter-space doctrines. The U.S. has established a Space Force. Russia operates mobile ASAT units. China's space situational awareness program is tracking every object above the Asia-Pacific.

India has set up its Defence Space Agency, tasked with integrating air, space, and cyber into a coherent grid.

The walls of air defence must now extend into the vacuum.

Emerging Response

To adapt to the space threat, air defence systems must evolve in five key areas:

Space Domain Awareness: Nations must know what is above them, who controls it, and how it might be used. India's upcoming NETRA satellite-based surveillance and ground telescopes are early steps in this direction.

Integrated Space Command Links: Future air defence decisions will be based not just on radar, but on orbital threat data—identifying whether a signal jamming radar is coming from a hilltop or a low-orbit satellite.

Anti-Satellite Interceptors: Just as aircraft are intercepted, hostile space assets must be neutralised when they pose a credible threat. These may not be kinetic—they could be laser dazzlers, jam signals, or deploy chaff clouds to confuse targeting.

Hardened Ground Systems: Radar domes, C2 centres, and missile units must be shielded not just from missiles but from directed energy and GPS-denial attacks from space.

Low-Orbit Defensive Constellations: India, the U.S., and others are exploring small-satellite constellations that can defend larger assets, relay signals, and act as orbital EW platforms—essentially creating miniature AD grids in orbit.

A Two-Front Sky

In the wars of the future, air defence will not fight on one front.

It must look horizontally for drones, aircraft, and cruise missiles. And it must look vertically for orbital jamming, satellite surveillance, and hypersonic precision weapons that drop from above like thunderbolts.

Every AD commander will need a sky chart, a threat cloud, and a battle plan that extends to the stars. The upper sky is no longer neutral. It is militarised, monitored, and increasingly weaponised.

The once-theoretical "high ground" is now very real. And those who do not defend it may lose everything below it.

CHAPTER 18

◆◆◆

Space Forces and the New Air Defence Frontier

Once the sky became the floor of a higher battlefield, the old architecture of land-based air defence began to fray at the top.

Militaries across the world have responded by raising their eyes—and their commands—to space.

These Space Commands aren't just about defending satellites. They manage early warning systems for missile launches, coordinate satellite communication and ISR (Intelligence, Surveillance, Reconnaissance), oversee anti-satellite (ASAT) operations, and increasingly, feed real-time threat data into air defence networks.

Space Commands now act as the eyes and ears of air defence systems, watching from orbit and ensuring that no hostile action goes unnoticed or unanswered.

U.S. Space Force: Born out of Necessity

In 2019, the United States officially established the U.S. Space Force (USSF)—the first new military branch since 1947. It evolved from the U.S. Space Command, a unified combatant command responsible for military operations in the space domain.

Why?

Because China and Russia were developing ASAT missiles and satellite jammers. The battlefield was becoming networked through satellites, and future wars, including those involving air defence, would depend on space-based sensors and communication.

The USSF today operates SBIRS satellites that provide real-time missile launch warnings, manages satellite constellations used for global air defence coordination, and works closely with NORAD and MDA to link orbital data to ground-based interceptors.

For every Patriot battery on the ground, there's a silent satellite feeding it a heat signature from thousands of kilometres above.

Russia's Aerospace Forces: Merging Air and Space

Russia anticipated this integration early. In 2015, it merged its Air Force and Space Forces into a single branch: the Russian Aerospace Forces (VKS).

Under VKS, Russia operates early warning satellites and ground radars as a combined command, controls strategic anti-satellite assets (e.g., Nudol interceptor), and develops S-500 systems, advertised to target satellites and ballistic missiles.

This consolidation reflects a doctrine where air and space are seen as one continuous theatre, requiring a unified defence strategy.

China: A Silent Ascent

China's military space efforts are wrapped in opacity, but in 2015, it created the People's Liberation Army Strategic Support Force (PLASSF)—a hybrid entity covering space warfare, cyber operations, and electronic warfare.

The PLASSF oversees satellite launches, orbital ISR, development of ASAT missiles and lasers, and the disruption of enemy command and control.

China's Yaogan series of satellites supports real-time tracking of global air activity, giving its AD systems a clearer picture of the aerial threat domain than ever before.

India's Defence Space Command: A Strategic Lift-Off

India's journey into military space began with civilian launches by ISRO (Indian Space Research Organisation), defence inputs via RISAT and Cartosat satellite families, and the 2019 Mission Shakti, a successful ASAT test.

ASAT being displayed during the Republic Day Parade, 2020

Following this, India established its own Defence Space Agency (DSA)—the precursor to a fully-fledged Defence Space Command.

Under DSA, India has set up space situational awareness infrastructure, created links between IACCS (Integrated Air Command and Control System) and space-derived inputs, and begun coordinating military satellite operations, like GSAT-7A and GSAT-6A used for air force communications.

The aim is to evolve DSA into a tri-service Defence Space Command, likely parallel to the U.S. model, but adapted to Indian constraints.

Space's Role in Air Defence: The Five Frontline Functions

Space Commands now directly impact air defence operations through:

Missile Early Warning

Satellites detect IR signatures from missile launches faster than any ground radar.

India is developing this through projects like Netra and DRDO's planned IR satellites.

Space Commands

US.	Russia	China	India

U.S. Space Command (SPACECOM) 2019 Scope • Satellite operations • Missile warning • Space control Capabilities • Early warning satellites • SBIRS • GSSAP	**Russian Aerospoace Forces (VKS) 2015** Scope • Military satellites • ASAT weapons • Space surveillance Capabilities • Early warning satellites • PL-19 Nudol ASAT missile • Plesetsk Cosmodrome	**PLA Strategic Support Force (SSF) 2015** Scope • Military satellites • ASAT weapons • Electronic warfare Capabilities • Early warning satellites • SC-19 and DN series ASAT missile • Yaogan ISR satellites	**Defense Space Agency (DSA) 2019** Scope • Military satellites • ASAT weapons • Space operations Capabilities • Early warning • Mission Shakti test • GSAT-7A (Rukmini)

Precision Targeting and Tracking

ISR satellites feed coordinates into AD networks for cueing interceptors.

Communication Resilience

Satellites ensure AD units stay connected even if ground lines are jammed or destroyed.

ASAT Threat Response

If enemy satellites are providing kill-chain intelligence, Space Commands must neutralise or jam them.

Electronic Intelligence and Spectrum Mapping

Monitoring enemy radar emissions and jamming activity from orbit allows air defence to prepare or evade in real time.

The New Doctrine: Air Defence with an Orbital Spine

Tomorrow's air defence is being written today by officers who command space fleets, not missile brigades.

The doctrine is clear. No missile will be fired without orbital confirmation. No radar warning will be trusted without satellite correlation. No AD bubble will be secure unless its overhead sensors are hardened.

In India, the challenge is to expand its military satellite fleet, integrate civilian and military space assets, and transition from reactive surveillance to proactive denial.

A formalised Defence Space Command, staffed by all three services and embedded with ISRO and DRDO liaisons, will be critical to raising the ceiling of Indian air defence—from the clouds to the cosmos.

Space is no longer just a high ground—it is the first frontier of defence. And the commanders who master it will not only defend their nations from the sky.

They will own the sky itself.

CHAPTER 19

◆◆◆

The Machine Decides—AI & Cyber in Air Defence

The sky has always been fast, but now it is too fast for humans alone. When missiles travel at Mach 10, drones swarm by the hundreds, and threats emerge not in hours but in milliseconds, air defence is undergoing a quiet but profound transformation. At the heart of this shift is a new operator—not a seasoned radar controller or a fighter pilot, but a machine learning algorithm trained to see, decide, and act.

Artificial Intelligence has begun to reshape every layer of air defence, from early warning to target prioritisation, from fire control to post-strike assessment. In traditional systems, the sequence from detection to interception moved through a chain of human judgment: someone saw, someone evaluated, and someone fired. But with AI, the system itself learns to distinguish a bird from a drone, a decoy from a real missile, and a threat from a distraction. It does so not just faster, but often more accurately, drawing from vast libraries of historical radar signatures and combat simulations.

Modern AI-powered radars now adapt to clutter, shift frequencies in real time, and prioritise signals based on predictive analysis. In command centres, AI engines fuse data from satellites, ground sensors, airborne platforms, and human intelligence into a single, constantly updating picture of the sky. Threats are scored, engagements are sequenced, and responses are simulated before action is taken. In some cases, the machine does not ask. It simply informs: this is the optimal course of action.

In live exercises, AI has already proven its edge. During a trial in the Western Air Force, an AI fire-control system outperformed experienced officers in intercepting a complex mix of drones and cruise missiles, achieving higher hit probabilities and faster response times. The Indian Air Force has also begun integrating AI into IACCS, allowing for predictive radar cueing, dynamic rerouting of aircraft, and faster relaying of threats across commands.

But with this speed and efficiency comes a new kind of uncertainty. What happens when AI makes a wrong call? Who is accountable if a machine locks onto a civilian aircraft misidentified as a loitering munition? As decision cycles shrink from minutes to milliseconds, the role of the human commander becomes paradoxical: both more crucial and more removed. The challenge is not just to build smarter systems, but to ensure that those systems remain under meaningful human control.

◆◆◆

AI also raises the stakes in electronic warfare. In the past, jamming confused machines; now, machines adapt. Adversaries will develop counter-AI measures—spoofing, deception, and even AI hunters trained to anticipate and exploit patterns. The battle will not just be of metal and fuel, but of algorithms fighting algorithms in stealth and speed.

Despite these dilemmas, the direction is clear. AI is no longer an add-on. It is becoming the architecture. In future air defence grids, AI may select the interceptor, chart its trajectory, hand off the target from radar to missile, and issue a post-engagement report, all without waiting for permission. Humans will set the rules, perhaps, but the war in the sky will be fought by learning machines trained not just to destroy, but to decide.

Yes, while much of the use of AI in air defence remains classified or embedded within broader systems, several real-world developments have highlighted how AI is increasingly influencing the battlefield, especially in air defence scenarios.

AI in the Iron Dome (2021 Gaza Conflict)

During the May 2021 conflict between Israel and Hamas, over 4,300 rockets were fired at Israeli cities in under 11 days. The Iron Dome system, long known for its accuracy, achieved a reported interception rate of 90%—despite unprecedented saturation and tactical unpredictability.

What was less publicised—but later acknowledged—was Iron Dome's use of machine learning algorithms that allowed it to dynamically prioritise targets. The AI component analysed in real time which rockets posed the greatest threat to civilian areas, and allowed the system to ignore those headed for open fields, thereby conserving interceptors and ensuring a response to real danger.

In essence, the AI didn't just track; it decided who to save. And it did so at a pace and scale no human command post could match.

NATO's Dragonfly Program (Ongoing Trials)

NATO has been experimenting with the Dragonfly Project, which involves AI-guided interceptor drones designed to neutralise other UAVs mid-air. In recent exercises in Estonia and Poland, the AI engines successfully detected, tracked, and autonomously intercepted low-flying drone targets simulating loitering munitions.

The breakthrough was not just in target engagement, but in the AI's ability to distinguish decoys from real threats, thanks to a machine-learning model trained on thousands of drone flight profiles.

This type of autonomous decision-making marks a shift in short-range air defence, particularly in drone-heavy conflict zones.

India's Project Trinetra: AI in Airspace Surveillance

While still developing, India's Project Trinetra is an example of homegrown AI in military command and control. Integrated into IACCS nodes, Trinetra fuses inputs from airborne early warning systems, radar, and electronic intelligence to predict the likely path of unidentified aerial contacts, even when those objects are flying "dark" or using deceptive manoeuvres.

In at least one reported instance along India's western front, Trinetra helped reclassify a suspicious radar contact as a flock of birds caught in a thermal current, preventing the scramble of fighters—a real-world example of how AI can prevent wasteful or dangerous overreaction.

◆◆◆

These stories point to a future where AI will no longer be a behind-the-scenes analyst—it will be a decision-maker in the air defence kill chain. And as these systems mature, the ethical, strategic, and operational implications will deepen.

In a sky where threats evolve faster than thought, AI offers a way to keep up. But it also changes the meaning of readiness. No longer is it just a matter of alert crews and sharpened missiles. It is now a question of data, training sets, and trust—trust that the machine watching the sky will know when to act, and when to wait. That trust may become the most valuable shield of all.

Cyber Is Now a Flight Path

Air defence systems are digital, and digital means hackable. Yes, the cyber domain has a deep and growing bearing on air defence.

Once thought of as distinct spheres—missiles in the sky, malware in the server—the lines between kinetic warfare and cyber warfare have blurred beyond recognition. Today, an air defence system may not be brought down by an enemy aircraft or overwhelmed by a missile barrage. It may be disabled by a keystroke.

At the heart of modern air defence lies a dense web of digital systems: radar arrays, communication relays, fire-control computers, satellite uplinks, and command networks that stretch across services and borders. Each node in this network is a potential point of vulnerability. If even one link is compromised, the entire system risks delay, misdirection, or paralysis. The cyber domain, in this context, is not just a new battlefield—it is the bloodstream of all others.

There have been real-world glimpses of this convergence. In 2007, a suspected cyberattack on Syrian radar systems reportedly blinded them moments before Israeli aircraft struck a suspected nuclear facility. In Ukraine, Russian cyber operations have routinely targeted radar and missile warning systems, not by jamming them from the air but by infiltrating their backend through corrupted software updates and phishing campaigns. And in 2015, U.S. intelligence revealed that Chinese hackers had exfiltrated technical data on advanced American missile defence systems, including components of the THAAD and Patriot systems.

◆◆◆

For India, the stakes are rising. As systems like IACCS, Netra, and BMD become increasingly digitised, they also become increasingly exposed. The very strengths of networked air defence—speed, integration, and reach—also make them vulnerable to false signals, malware injections, and data corruption. A spoofed radar contact can trigger an unnecessary launch. A denial-of-service attack can stall target tracking during a real threat. A corrupted missile firmware update can render a strategic battery useless in wartime.

◆◆◆

Defending against these threats is not as simple as erecting a firewall. It requires layered cyber hygiene across the entire supply chain, from procurement to deployment. It demands that every air defence operator be trained not only to track the sky but to suspect the system. It also requires developing resilient protocols for degraded operations—ways to fight even when screens go dark, or commands fail to send.

◆◆◆

The cyber domain does not replace the air. But it seeps into every sensor, every trigger, every relay that links a warning to a weapon.

In the age of digital warfare, air defence is not only about what we can see above us. It is also about what might be happening, silently, below the surface—between circuits, across networks, and inside the code. The most dangerous sky may not be the one overhead, but the one inside the system.

Future AD will require quantum-encrypted communication, resilient mesh networks, and autonomous fallback modes in case of cyber disruption.

◆◆◆

In the end, air defence may not remain a set of platforms or regiments. It may evolve into a pervasive sensory grid, an autonomous neural net humming in the sky, identifying, adapting, and reacting faster than any adversary can plan.

It will not just stop threats. It will predict, prevent, and pre-empt. This is the shield of the future.

CHAPTER 20

◆◆◆

The Human in Air Defence—How Stanislav Petrov Saved the World

The human element in air defence is both the oldest component and the least replaceable.

Technology may have transformed the sky into a digital battlespace of radars, missiles, interceptors, and command nodes—and autonomous AI may well be on its way—but at least for now, behind every alert, every launch, every split-second decision, there is still a person. Sometimes a watch officer with a headset. Sometimes a pilot at 40,000 feet. Sometimes a technician reading a ghost signal at 3 AM.

They are the ones who must do what machines cannot: interpret, hesitate, override, and sometimes disobey. Air defence is full of such moments—unspectacular yet sacred—when a finger hovers, not presses.

You can automate the detection. You can automate the kill. But only a human can say: "not yet."

In the sterile glow of an air defence control room, operators don't look heroic. They wear headsets, not helmets. Their screens flicker with waveforms and signatures, not explosions.

Yet their job is brutal in its demands: to remain vigilant even when nothing happens. For hours. For days. And then—within 30 seconds—make a decision that may launch a missile worth ₹50 lakh at a blip that turns out to be a weather balloon.

This is what they call the "watcher's burden". It is not about shooting. It is about knowing when not to shoot. And when to act before it's too late. In air defence, errors rarely come from ignorance. They come from fatigue, from the pressure of holding life-or-death decisions inside a dull hum of routine.

Despite automation, almost every advanced air defence system still insists on a "man in the loop." That is, a human must confirm the launch, especially when the stakes are high, or the target is ambiguous.

Interceptors are not flown by code. They're flown by people who must identify threats in seconds, in weather, at night, while moving at Mach speeds. Sometimes they must pursue. Sometimes they must turn back.

In the Mi-17 friendly fire incident in 2019, the absence of a clear human override led to tragedy—a harsh reminder that judgment must not only be present, but also trusted.

Machines calculate; humans discern. No AI yet built has matched that blend of instinct, intuition, and accountability. The future may promise autonomous kill chains. But every military ethics panel insists: a human must remain in control of lethal decisions, especially when a civilian aircraft goes off-route, a hijacking code is misread, or a drone enters restricted airspace during peacetime. Because in these moments, what is required is not just a technical response but a moral pause.

The best systems don't replace the human—they support them. They filter out noise, suggest responses, and provide confidence intervals. But in the end, it is still a person in uniform who confirms the launch code, scans the sky, or radios a warning. They do so not for glory, but out of a silent compact: "Let nothing through. Let no one die on my watch. But let no one be killed unless I know they must be."

That is the soul of air defence. Not just sensors, not just missiles—but the human standing between radar and ruin.

26 September 1983 – A Night Like No Other

It was just past midnight when Lieutenant Colonel Stanislav Petrov reported for duty at Serpukhov-15, a top-secret Soviet bunker buried deep in a forest south of Moscow.

Petrov was not a general. Not a politician. Just a mid-ranking officer in the Soviet Air Defence Forces assigned to a specific, terrifying task: monitoring Oko, the Soviet Union's early-warning satellite system, built to detect intercontinental ballistic missile (ICBM) launches from the United States.

He sat in front of a screen. Behind him, walls of computers hummed. Fluorescent lights cast a pale glow. The Cold War was at one of its tensest moments—just weeks earlier, Soviet jets had shot down a South Korean airliner (KAL 007), killing all 269 people on board, including a U.S. Congressman. NATO was about to conduct a massive military exercise (Able Archer 83), and the Soviet high command feared it might be a cover for a surprise nuclear strike.

Tension was not theoretical. It was daily, ambient, and electric. And then the siren wailed.

◆◆◆

Petrov turned to his screen. The computer display flashed a word no one wanted to see:

"LAUNCH"

According to the satellite system, a single missile had been launched from an American silo.

Petrov froze. He knew what the protocol demanded:

Pick up the hotline.

Report the launch to higher command.

Trigger the possibility of a retaliatory nuclear strike.

But he hesitated.

"Just one missile?" he thought. That didn't make sense. If the U.S. were launching a first strike, it wouldn't be a single missile. It would be a full barrage.

He told his staff: "The system is probably malfunctioning." He waited.

And then came the second alert.

And the third.

And the fourth.

And the fifth.

Five American ICBMs now showed as airborne, inbound, and targeting the Soviet Union.

◆◆◆

Petrov knew the doctrine: a five-missile salvo could be a decapitation strike, aimed at blinding Soviet leadership before a full-scale attack.

His subordinates looked at him. His hands trembled. The phone was within reach. The clock ticked.

By all procedures, he should have reported the alert up the chain. Soviet policy was to respond immediately if an American attack was detected. The counterstrike would involve hundreds of nuclear missiles, aimed at U.S. cities and bases. It would be irreversible.

But Petrov didn't believe it. His gut said no. His mind said wait. He chose to violate protocol. He reported the alert as a false alarm.

Then he waited for impact.

Five minutes.

Ten minutes.

Nothing.

No explosions. No shockwaves. No mushroom clouds. Just silence.

The system had been wrong. The world had been five minutes from ending.

And Stanislav Petrov had saved it—not with a missile, but with a refusal.

◆◆◆

Investigators later discovered that the Soviet Oko satellite system had mistaken sunlight reflecting off high-altitude clouds over the U.S. missile fields as launches. A rare orbital geometry had created a false signal.

The radar systems, which would have confirmed or disproved the satellite data, had not yet picked up anything—Petrov had nothing but incomplete data and his own instincts.

And that's all it took.

Had someone else been on duty—a less sceptical officer, someone more by-the-book—the Soviet response could have been automatic. The U.S., detecting a nuclear launch, would have responded in kind.

Billions might have died.

(Source: Wikipedia)

Petrov was neither hailed as a hero nor punished. The incident was classified for years. When it finally became public in the late 1990s, the world reacted with awe, gratitude, and disbelief.

Petrov lived in quiet retirement outside Moscow. His house was modest, his demeanour unassuming. He gave a few interviews and was always reluctant. In one, when asked if he thought he had saved the world, he shrugged:

"That was my job. But yes... perhaps I did."

In 2006, he was honoured by the United Nations. In 2013, he received the Dresden Peace Prize. Petrov died in May 2017. A 2014 documentary, *The Man Who Saved the World*, told his story. In response to news of Petrov's death, Rep. Adam Schiff tweeted,

"Times of nuclear tension call for careful restraint. You may not know Stanislav Petrov, but at the height of the Cold War, he saved the world."

Why Petrov's Story Matters in Air Defence

His decision was not just a Cold War story. It is a permanent reminder of the human role in air defence.

He had:

A warning.

A system that said fire.

A doctrine that said act.

And a conscience that said wait.

Today, as systems become more autonomous, more dependent on AI, and faster in response, Petrov's moment becomes even more vital to remember.

Not every blinking light should trigger a war.

Sometimes, the greatest hero in air defence is the one who holds the line—and holds back.

CHAPTER 21

◆◆◆

The Civilian in Air Defence

In war, military air defences watch the sky to protect command posts, weapons silos, and strategic infrastructure. But increasingly, the sky threatens more than soldiers—it threatens cities, power grids, airports, and people in their homes. That is where civilian air defence comes in.

Not with missiles or radars, but with warning systems, public protocols, shelters, and silent coordination between civilian and military authorities.

If military air defence protects national power, civilian air defence protects the national psyche.

◆◆◆

The first large-scale civilian air defence systems emerged during World War II, when air raids over London, Berlin, and Tokyo made it clear that wars were no longer fought only on battlefields.

Air raid sirens, public drills, blackout policies, and community wardens and underground sheltering became routine. In Cold War-era America and the Soviet Union, civil defence added evacuation plans, radiation-proof bunkers, and public service announcements on how to survive a nuclear blast.

These systems were as psychological as they were practical, offering a sense of order under the looming threat of chaos.

Today, the line between military and civilian AD is blurred. Rockets from Gaza trigger Iron Dome launches over Tel Aviv, and simultaneous civilian app alerts and sirens. Russia's missile barrages on Kyiv lead to metro station evacuations, shelter drills, and public communications via encrypted apps. In Japan, J-Alert systems warn citizens of potential North Korean missile overflights.

The guiding principle is speed: "Get the warning to the public before the blast reaches them, or warn them it's not real at all."

India's Civilian Air Defence Reality

India's civilian air defence infrastructure has evolved, but remains under-discussed. It exists quietly, primarily under the Civil Defence Organisation (CDO) under the Ministry of Home Affairs (MHA), the state-level disaster management authorities, and the military-civil coordination cells in border districts and conflict-prone zones.

In Jammu and Kashmir, Punjab, and Arunachal Pradesh, where villagers live within the range of cross-border shelling or drone incursions, siren drills and evacuation procedures are occasionally rehearsed.

In major cities, the framework is largely reactive and embedded into NDMA (National Disaster Management Authority) protocols, with mock drills for CBRN (Chemical, Biological, Radiological, and Nuclear) threats, but little public knowledge of what to do in case of an aerial attack.

Unlike Israel or South Korea, India lacks automated early warning apps tied to AD networks, community shelters in urban zones, and public awareness campaigns on aerial threat protocols.

That said, the Ministry of Defence (MoD) and MHA have initiated pilot programs for integrating civil alerts into IACCS for border populations and developing text-based push alerts in the event of airspace violations or missile strikes.

The Modern Civilian Shield: Where It Needs to Go

In an age of loitering munitions, drone swarms, surgical airstrikes, and cyber attacks disrupting radar feeds, civilian air defence must evolve beyond sirens and slogans. It must include real-time public alert apps (linked to IAF's radar grid), digitally marked community shelters, QR-coded evacuation instructions in public places, and bi-directional communication between local authorities and defence ops rooms.

Even AI-based public address systems are being trialed globally—where the system speaks not just loudly, but clearly, with tailored instructions based on proximity to threat.

◆◆◆

Air defence is no longer a war between missiles. It is a war between signals, sensors, and seconds.

In those seconds, a civilian who knows what to do is part of the defence network. A civilian who doesn't is a casualty waiting to happen.

To prepare a country for aerial threats is not just to install missiles. It is to teach people what the first flash of light means, and what not to trust on a jamming-spoofed phone screen.

In India, with its massive population and increasing exposure to airspace conflicts, the invisible frontier is not in the sky. It's in the minds of the people standing under it.

CHAPTER 22

◆◆◆

Simulators, Wargaming, and Training in Air Defence

The warfighter's first battlefield is not the sky—it's the simulator screen.

Air defence, perhaps more than any other combat domain, demands instant decisions. A radar picks up a contact. A second passes. Is it a flock of birds or a loitering munition? An approaching C-130 or an F-16 on strike?

You don't have time to learn. You act based on what you've already internalised.

That's why training in air defence is not just technical—it's neurological. It rewires instinct. It builds mental reflexes. And it does so in a place where missiles aren't fired, enemies don't die, and yet every decision counts: the world of simulators and wargames.

Simulators: The Synthetic Battlefield

In India, as in most modern militaries, a majority of air defence training happens inside rooms filled with screens, joysticks, and threat matrices.

At institutions like the Army Air Defence College (AADC) in Gopalpur and IAF's Air Defence College in Lucknow, soldiers and officers sit in full-scale mock-ups of radar stations, command and control bunkers, SAM battery consoles, MANPADS fire units, and fighter-interceptor control suites.

Here, every variable can be controlled. The terrain can be a flat desert or high-altitude snow. The radar screen can show a Mirage 2000 or a swarm of micro-drones. Communications can be clear or jammed, and threats can be real or ghosts, symmetric or asymmetric.

The goal? Not perfection. But pattern recognition. Judgment under stress. And the muscle memory to act before a missile arrives.

Modern simulators incorporate 3D visualisation of radar and electro-optical feeds, and AI-controlled adversaries, capable of unpredictable manoeuvres. There are multiplayer networked drills, where different teams train simultaneously—radar crews in Rajasthan coordinating with interceptor pilots over a virtual Punjab

They also train errors deliberately. The Mi-17 friendly fire incident has been recreated in multiple drills. So has the 1979 NORAD false alarm scenario. Officers are graded on their ability to distinguish between noise and signal, bluff and battle. Because often in air defence, the first failure is the last.

Wargaming: Strategy Before Strategy

Beyond button-pressing drills lie the tabletop wargames—where air defence officers act as blue force defenders, red force attackers, or neutral referees.

At the College of Air Warfare, Secunderabad, and in joint Army-IAF exercises, wargames are used to model saturation strikes and swarm attacks, plan air defence for advancing formations, and test hypothetical deployments of new systems like S-400 or QRSAM. There are simulated joint operations with naval and space-based assets.

In these rooms, India fights wars that never happen, but must be ready for.

Integrated Live Exercises

India now routinely holds live-fire air defence drills, such as Vayu Shakti (IAF) and Surya Kiran (joint force). Missile tests from Akash, SPYDER, Igla, and Barak are routinely carried out, as are drone shootdowns over Pokhran and Ladakh, as well as exercises involving fighter controllers tracking hostile UAVs. These are where the synthetic meets the real, and the trained reflex is tested in the open sky.

Training the Human, Not Just the System

While weapons get smarter, humans remain at the core. That's why training also includes:

Cognitive load training: How to function during overwhelming saturation

EW disruption drills: Working under jamming and radar blindness

Rules of engagement training: Especially for intercepts in civilian airspace

Even ethical judgment is rehearsed:

When is it right to fire on an ambiguous radar contact near a civilian corridor?

How long can you wait before it's too late to act?

The right answer is often not taught. It is tested.

The coming decade will introduce holographic combat simulations, blending AR/VR (Augmented Reality/Virtual Reality) for multi-domain immersion, digital twins of entire AD grids, allowing real-time performance replay and correction. There will be AI instructors who will watch how you respond and adjust threat patterns to push your limits. Joint drone combat arenas, where soldiers train to use autonomous UAVs against enemy drones mid-air, will be common.

Because future air defence won't just be about hitting targets—it will be about outthinking adaptive threats.

◆◆◆

Air defence is a profession where you cannot wait to learn on the job. The soldier behind the console, the pilot in the cockpit, and the officer at the radar screen are all trained not just to react, but to rehearse every outcome before it arrives.

The missiles may be expensive.

But the wrong decision in five seconds costs more.

So militaries rehearse—not for spectacle, but for survival. Not because they know what the enemy will do, but because they cannot afford not to be ready when they do.

CHAPTER 23

◆◆◆

Legal, Ethical, and Diplomatic Aspects of Air Defence

At the heart of air defence lies a deceptively simple question: What are you defending, exactly?

You can defend the skies with missiles. But you must justify your defence with rules. And rules, unlike missiles, do not always fly straight.

Under international law, every nation has complete sovereignty over the airspace above its territory, extending vertically from the surface upward into the "navigable airspace." But where that space ends—and where outer space begins—remains ambiguously defined.

There is no universally agreed-upon ceiling. Practically, airspace is considered to end around 100 kilometres (the Kármán Line), but many defence engagements happen well below that. This creates a grey zone, especially when satellites pass overhead or missiles arc near exoatmospheric trajectories.

When air defence systems operate near these thresholds, what is permissible and what is provocative becomes a matter of interpretation and intent.

The Rules of Engagement (RoE)

Who Can You Shoot, and When?

Air defence operators often face split-second decisions, but the consequences are bound by international humanitarian law (IHL) and rules of engagement:

Distinction: Is the object military or civilian?

Proportionality: Will the intercept cause more harm than the original threat?

Necessity: Is the threat imminent and unavoidable?

Accountability: Can the decision be justified after the fact?

In conflicts like the Gulf War, Kosovo, Syria, and Ukraine, air defence errors have killed civilians, downed airliners, and triggered global outrage. The 2020 Iranian downing of Ukrainian International Airlines Flight 752—mistaken for a hostile target—highlighted how a single AD decision can become a diplomatic firestorm.

Civilian Aircraft and AD Protocols

Modern air defence must coexist with civil aviation. This leads to complex legal obligations

The Chicago Convention (1944) prohibits the use of weapons against civilian aircraft. Annex 17 of ICAO (International Civil Aviation Organization) mandates early warning protocols and flight information sharing.

Yet incidents continue to occur. Korean Air Flight 007 (1983) was shot down by the Soviet Union, as was Iran Air Flight 655 (1988), which was destroyed by a U.S. Navy missile.

India's AD systems in Jammu and Punjab often operate under layered coordination with civilian ATC to avoid escalation or tragic error.

Still, fog of war, radar ambiguity, or doctrine failures can override policy in seconds.

Defence and International Law: A Shifting Terrain

Unlike nuclear weapons or landmines, air defence systems are not heavily regulated under global treaties.

There is no international agreement prohibiting the deployment of anti-air or anti-missile systems near borders, or the use of air defence against spaceborne assets (though ASAT tests have drawn scrutiny), or on hard-kill measures against drones that violate airspace.

Instead, diplomacy works through customary law, bilateral understandings, and UN (United Nations) Security Council warnings.

India's deployment of the S-400 system near China and Pakistan borders, for instance, is not illegal, but it is politically sensitive and watched closely by foreign observers.

Ethical Dilemmas in Air Defence

Modern air defence systems are increasingly autonomous. This raises urgent ethical questions:

If an AI-controlled system misidentifies a target, who is responsible?

Is it ethical to deploy interceptors in urban areas, knowing the debris risk?

When shooting down a suspected drone, what if it turns out to be civilian or medical?

Many militaries, including India's, now embed "human-in-the-loop" safeguards—but as threats get faster, these safeguards are under stress.

The ethical challenge is no longer just about whom to shoot, but also when not to shoot, and how much to trust a machine.

Diplomacy in the Sky

Air defence is often used as a tool of diplomacy. Patriot systems in Poland signal NATO resolve, while the Iron Dome exports are wrapped in defence partnerships. India's purchase of the S-400 from Russia strained ties with the U.S., triggering CAATSA (Countering America's Adversaries Through Sanctions Act) waiver debates.

In 21st-century geopolitics, selling a SAM system is like selling influence. And shooting one is like ringing a bell that cannot be unrung.

At the same time, confidence-building measures (CBMs) like hotlines, flight notification protocols, and airspace use agreements have become essential to prevent miscalculations.

Future: Governance of the Electromagnetic Sky

As air defence evolves to include directed energy weapons, anti-satellite systems, electromagnetic jammers and spoofers and AI-enabled autonomous interceptors, the need for legal frameworks, shared ethics, and multilateral diplomacy becomes urgent.

Should there be a Geneva Convention for drones and loitering munitions?

Who verifies AD systems' compliance with proportionality in real time?

Can AI weapons ever be held to legal standards?

These are no longer abstract debates. They are pressing realities, because the sky has become both a domain of war and a realm of law.

The Law Above Us All

Air defence does not operate in a vacuum. Every missile launched upward travels through a web of legal obligations, ethical boundaries, and diplomatic implications.

The radar operator sees a blip.

But behind that blip is a chain of responsibility—stretching from a console to a courtroom, from a battalion to a nation's image.

Missiles fall in seconds.

But trust, reputation, and legality fall over decades—and rise even slower.

PART II

THE INTERLUDES

Some Interesting Facets of Air Defence Compiled for the Curious Reader

CHAPTER 24

◆◆◆

Interlude I: Yom Kippur (1973) and Balakot (2019)

Let us look at two decisive air battles—Yom Kippur (1973) and Balakot (2019)—that make ideal case studies in understanding AD. The former marks a turning point in networked, radar-guided air defence warfare, while the latter is a crisp, modern-day encounter between nuclear-armed rivals using both kinetic and information warfare tactics. Each story, though different in scope, offers essential insights into how air defence plays out under fire.

Fire over the Sinai – The Yom Kippur War, 1973

> For the first time, air superiority was denied to the Israelis. The lesson was brutal: fly low, die early.

On the afternoon of October 6, 1973, as Israelis observed Yom Kippur—the holiest day in the Jewish calendar—waves of Egyptian and Syrian forces launched a surprise attack on Israeli-held territory.

But what shocked Israeli commanders more than the ground assault was this: their invincible air force was suddenly taking unsustainable losses.

The reason? A wall of Soviet-made air defence systems—SAM-2s, SAM-3s, and most devastatingly, the highly mobile SAM-6 (Kvadrat). These were not isolated batteries. They were linked, layered, and constantly on the move.

The Israeli Air Force had been trained on the success of the 1967 Six-Day War, where it had destroyed enemy aircraft on the ground and ruled the skies. But in 1973, it tried the same tactics—and lost nearly 40 aircraft in just two days.

Every time an Israeli Phantom or Mirage entered Egyptian airspace, it triggered a coordinated air defence response. Long-range radars picked them up 100 kilometres away, while the mid-range SAMs locked on as they approached the canal. Low-flying jets were hit by short-range missiles and ZSU-23-4 Shilka guns.

Pilots tried flying under the radar. But the Egyptians had created kill zones just above treetop level. As one Israeli pilot radioed before ejecting: "They're everywhere. We're blind. Even when we see them, they've already fired."

What made this war different was not just the missile count—it was the coordination. Egypt and Syria, with Soviet advisors, had built what we now call an Integrated Air Defence System (IADS). For the first time, radars were linked to command centres, missile batteries were mobile and repositioned every few hours, while electronic countermeasures were deployed to jam Israeli comms.

It wasn't just brute force. It was smart. It was flexible. And it changed air warfare forever.

The U.S. and NATO, watching from the sidelines, took copious notes. Israel itself adapted quickly, sending in F-4 Phantoms on "wild weasel" missions to suppress enemy air defences (SEAD)—a term that entered air combat doctrine after this war.

Yom Kippur War taught the world that air superiority could no longer be assumed—it had to be earned, and defended, every second. The sky had become a contested, lethal zone, layered with missiles, radars, and firepower. Modern air defence was no longer just about protecting cities. It could now reshape battle outcomes on the ground.

That principle would echo, decades later, over the Himalayas.

Shadows over Balakot – India and Pakistan, 2019

> No war was declared, but weapons were fired. Missiles were launched. Jets were downed. And radars blinked to life along one of the world's tensest borders.

On the morning of 26 February 2019, Indian Mirage 2000 jets crossed the Line of Control and struck a camp near Balakot in Pakistan's Khyber Pakhtunkhwa province. It was India's response to the Pulwama suicide bombing, which had killed 40 Indian paramilitary personnel.

The airstrike itself was brief. Precision-guided bombs were dropped. The jets turned back without contest. But the real test of air defence came the next morning.

Pakistan retaliated with a coordinated air operation on 27 February. Multiple F-16s, JF-17s, and Mirage IIIs approached the LoC in sectors from Jammu to Rajouri. Indian Su-30MKIs, MiG-21 Bisons, and Mirage 2000s scrambled to intercept.

Indian ground-based air defences and radar units lit up. Netra AEW&C aircraft guided IAF assets, while low-level tracking radars picked up Pakistani ingress. Command centres coordinated airspace deconfliction—a hard task, as both sides flew similar Russian-origin aircraft.

In the dogfight that followed, a Pakistani F-16 was reportedly downed (though Pakistan denies this), and an Indian MiG-21 Bison, piloted by Wing Commander Abhinandan Varthaman, was shot down and captured after crossing the LoC.

While no air defence missile was fired in this encounter, their presence loomed. Pakistan's LY-80 (HQ-16) medium-range SAMs tracked Indian aircraft from a distance. India's Akash batteries were on alert across northern airbases. Forward locations were reinforced with mobile QRSAM units and MANPADS.

This was one of the first real-world scenarios where both sides had nuclear weapons, and yet conventional air power and AD posture shaped the outcome.

The dogfight itself became symbolic, but radar coverage, networked response, and communication discipline prevented the situation from spiralling further.

◆◆◆

While the jets clashed in the skies over the Line of Control on the morning of 27 February 2019, another aircraft—a Mi-17 V5 helicopter—lifted off from Srinagar Air Force Station. Its flight was routine: a maintenance sortie, heading toward an ammunition depot just a few kilometres away.

Six minutes later, it was gone.

At 10.10 AM, the helicopter was shot down by an Indian SPYDER surface-to-air missile, launched from a base that had just gone on high alert due to incoming threats from Pakistan. All six IAF personnel on board and one civilian on the ground were killed.

At first, there was confusion. Was it engine failure? Sabotage? Enemy action?

The truth emerged slowly, and painfully. An IAF Court of Inquiry later confirmed it: the Mi-17 had been mistaken for a hostile aerial threat by its own side.

The helicopter's Identification Friend or Foe (IFF) system was reportedly turned off or not functioning. The airbase was in a state of heightened tension, with multiple unidentified radar contacts. A breakdown in command-level communication led the operators to believe the chopper was a threat. Within seconds of detection, the missile battery fired.

It wasn't malice, nor was it incompetence. It was the fog of war, amplified by technical blind spots and human fatigue. But the incident was more than a tragedy—it was a wake-up call. It exposed serious procedural lapses in AD operations, especially under pressure, forcing a review of IFF protocols, particularly for helicopters flying close to the front.

It also revealed how, in a networked battlespace, even one unverified dot on a radar can spiral into irreversible loss. In many ways, this one event became the inverse of the Balakot airstrike. If the strike symbolised precision and surprise, the Mi-17 shootdown embodied the risks of fractured situational awareness in a complex AD environment.

The lesson, air defence is not just about intercepting the enemy. It is about not intercepting your own. And in modern warfare—where milliseconds matter, and machines often make decisions faster than humans can double-check them—the greatest challenge for any air defence system is not simply reacting, but discerning.

CHAPTER 25

◆◆◆

Interlude II: Patriot vs Scud—The First Televised Missile Duel

The skies over Dhahran, Saudi Arabia, lit up just after midnight on 18 January 1991. Screaming across the night came a missile—long, lean, and Soviet-made. The Scud, fired from deep within Iraq, arced high into the stratosphere before plummeting toward the coalition base at King Abdulaziz Air Base. On its descent, the world held its breath. What would stop it?

Seconds later, another missile launched from the desert floor—a sleek white dart known as the Patriot. It raced upward with a tail of flame, veered sharply, and slammed into the descending Scud. The collision lit the sky with a sharp white bloom.

Cameras caught it. CNN beamed it across the globe. Cheers erupted across the base. For the first time in modern warfare, the world had watched a missile intercept another missile—live. This was not just a tactical moment. It was symbolic.

The Gulf War had become the world's first networked war, and the Patriot–Scud encounters were its most potent image—a battle between aggression and protection, between terror and technology.

The Rise of the Scud

The Scud was never meant to be accurate. It didn't need to be.

Born in the Soviet Union during the Cold War, it was a derivative of Germany's V-2 rocket: a ballistic missile capable of delivering a warhead hundreds of kilometres away in less than ten minutes. Its aim was to sow fear, not precision. Its flight path—a high arc followed by a steep plunge—was designed to make defence nearly impossible.

Iraq, under Saddam Hussein, had stockpiled Scuds and even developed extended-range variants like the Al-Hussein, capable of striking Riyadh and Tel Aviv from within its borders.

They were not smart weapons. But they were psychological weapons. They sent people scrambling to shelters, triggered chemical weapon fears, and created panic disproportionate to their actual blast yield.

And crucially, they could not be intercepted. At least, that was the belief until 1991.

Enter the Patriot

The Patriot missile system was originally designed by Raytheon in the 1970s, not to intercept ballistic missiles, but to protect against aircraft and cruise missiles. But by the late 1980s, with modifications and new guidance packages, it had been adapted for theatre ballistic missile defence.

In the run-up to the Gulf War, the U.S. deployed Patriot batteries in both Saudi Arabia and Israel. The message was clear: America would not only fight the war, it would protect its allies and its bases.

Each Patriot battery consisted of:

A radar unit to detect incoming threats.

A control station with operators ready to launch.

A launcher with up to 16 interceptor missiles, each costing over $1 million.

The system was fast, networked, and claimed to offer a chance—just a chance—to strike an incoming missile before it struck the ground.

The Intercepts Begin

Over the course of the Gulf War, Iraq launched over 80 Scud missiles. Most were aimed at Saudi Arabia. About 40 were targeted at Israel, in an attempt to provoke a response that might fracture the U.S.-led Arab coalition.

Patriot missiles responded again and again. The world watched from bunkers, newsrooms, and living rooms as white trails stitched the night sky.

People began to speak of Patriots not just as hardware, but as saviours. In Riyadh and Tel Aviv, they became symbols of defiance, of reassurance. There were even bumper stickers in Saudi Arabia that read: "My other car is a Patriot."

CNN's footage of Patriot intercepts—some successful, some not—became iconic. For the first time, air defence had a public face.

Here's what made the Patriot-Scud duels so unique. The Scud's re-entry phase lasted less than a minute, so the Patriot had a 10–20 second window to lock on, calculate trajectory, and fire. Since Scud missiles often broke apart in flight due to poor engineering, this confused radars, forcing operators to pick one target among many. Every Patriot launch was a million-dollar decision. If it failed, it could result in mass casualties. And Patriot failures weren't just military losses—they were public failures, watched by millions.

The U.S. military claimed a high intercept rate—up to 80% in Saudi Arabia and 50% in Israel. But later analysis by MIT and GAO (Government Accountability Office) suggested much lower success rates—perhaps only 10–25% true intercepts.

The Tragedy at Dhahran

On 25 February 1991, a Scud missile struck a U.S. Army barracks in Dhahran, Saudi Arabia, killing 28 American soldiers and wounding over 100 more.

The tragedy shook confidence in the Patriot system. Post-war investigation revealed that the Patriot software had drifted slightly over time, causing a miscalculation in the tracking algorithm. The system had not "seen" the Scud in time.

This single event became a painful reminder that even the best air defence systems have limits. It also triggered a wave of improvements in software maintenance, real-time calibration, and human override protocols.

Legacy: What the Gulf War Changed

Despite mixed performance, the Patriot-Scud battles left a profound legacy. They proved that missile defence was possible. Until then, most experts believed ballistic missile interception was science fiction. The Gulf War proved it was hard, but real.

They shifted the arms race. Post-war, countries like Israel, India, Japan, and South Korea accelerated investments in missile defence. They also created the first "publicly visible" air defence war. Today, systems like Iron Dome or S-400 are seen as strategic tools because the Gulf War taught the world how important perception is in defence.

The U.S. continued to upgrade Patriot systems, developed THAAD (Terminal High Altitude Area Defense), and began experimenting with hit-to-kill interceptors and space-based early warning systems. The Gulf War was no longer just a war of tanks and jets—it was a war of sensors, radars, computers, and missiles. In a sense, it marked the dawn of the modern networked battlespace, where air defence is no longer the last resort—it's the first response.

What people remember most isn't the radar cross-sections or algorithmic lags. They remember the sound of a Patriot launch—the deep rumble, the orange flare, the rush of hope. In shelters across Israel, families gathered with radios, praying that this time, the missile would miss.

In Saudi Arabia, soldiers ran drills between bunks and bunkers, always listening for the siren that came seconds before the sky lit up.

And somewhere, behind a screen, an operator watched a blip move across the scope, his finger hovering over the button, knowing that a delay of two seconds could change the course of a night. These were not cinematic moments. They were the everyday math of survival, carried out in dim rooms by young technicians and old machines.

Patriot vs Scud was never just a military engagement. It was a symbol of a turning point—when the world realised that defence had to become as agile, fast, and technological as offence.

In the years since, the systems have changed. The missiles are smarter. The radars are better. The interceptors now travel faster and think faster than ever before.

But the core drama remains unchanged.

A missile launches.

A siren wails.

And somewhere in the sky, another missile answers.

CHAPTER 26

◆◆◆

Interlude III: Israel's Iron Dome—The AD Role Model

Suddenly, the siren wails. You have 15 seconds. You run. You crouch. And then—nothing. Just a distant thud. Because the sky caught it.

On a warm May evening in 2021, the people of Tel Aviv sat at cafés, jogged along the boardwalk, and watched the sky turn gold. It was the kind of dusk that belongs on postcards. And then came the siren.

Within seconds, the soundscape of the city shifted. Footsteps quickened. Children were pulled close. In every neighbourhood, people dashed into stairwells, underpasses, and shelters. Above them, unseen and unheard, multiple rockets, launched from Gaza, hurtled toward the city at supersonic speeds. Each one carried enough firepower to turn a house into rubble, a café into ash. And then something happened—something that still feels like science fiction, though it is now a routine reality in Israel.

A single missile rose into the sky, tracing a near-vertical path. Then another. Then more. From hidden batteries and mobile trucks around the city's outskirts, a string of interceptors launched, tracked, and collided mid-air with the incoming rockets.

High above, white plumes curled like smoke rings in the dusky air. The explosions were distant, almost soft. When people emerged from their shelters, they found their streets untouched, their city still standing, and their lives intact.

This was Iron Dome, doing what no system had done before: turning the unpredictable chaos of short-range rocket fire into something that could be calmly, almost mathematically, denied.

◆◆◆

The Iron Dome did not come from comfort. It came from necessity. For years, towns like Sderot, Ashkelon, and Beersheba lived under the arc of frequent rocket fire from militant groups in Gaza. These weren't precision-guided missiles; they were Qassam rockets—cheap, crude, homemade, and devastatingly effective in one regard: psychological terror.

They arrived without warning, fired in salvos, and exploited the Achilles' heel of modern militaries: short-range saturation attacks, too fast for traditional systems to intercept, too erratic to predict, and too numerous to absorb.

In 2006, during the Second Lebanon War, over 4,000 rockets were launched into northern Israel by Hezbollah, forcing over a million people into shelters. The Israeli Defence Forces (IDF) had no real countermeasures. That war became the breaking point.

A year later, the Israeli Ministry of Defence awarded the defence firm Rafael Advanced Defense Systems a project that sounded impossible: build a system that could shoot down thousands of cheap rockets flying erratically at short ranges—and do it cheaply, fast, and under real-time civilian pressure.

Sceptics said it couldn't be done. But Israel did it. By 2011, Iron Dome was operational.

◆◆◆

At its core, Iron Dome is deceptively simple. It operates in three parts:

Detection and Tracking Radar
Scans the sky and identifies incoming threats.

Battle Management and Control (BMC)
Analyses trajectories to determine where each rocket is headed, and whether it's likely to strike a populated area.

Missile Firing Unit
If a rocket poses danger, a Tamir interceptor missile is launched to destroy it mid-air.

Here's the trick: Iron Dome doesn't shoot down every rocket. It ignores those projected to fall in open fields or the sea. It only engages those headed for homes, schools, and hospitals. This intelligent discrimination is why the system is so cost-effective and so admired. It doesn't just react—it calculates.

Each Tamir interceptor costs roughly $40,000 to $100,000, depending on configuration. That's steep, but less than the cost of a collapsed apartment block or mass evacuation. It's a high-stakes numbers game played in the air. And so far, Iron Dome has intercepted over 90% of the rockets it has targeted—a figure unheard of in missile defence history.

(Courtesy: US DoD website)

Tel Aviv was never the frontline. For years, it was distant enough from the southern borders that most rocket fire from Gaza couldn't reach it. That changed.

In conflicts such as *Operation Pillar of Defense* (2012), *Protective Edge* (2014), and most dramatically in May 2021, militant groups began launching longer-range variants, such as the Fajr-5 and M-75 rockets, capable of striking Israel's heartland.

The calculus changed. If Tel Aviv—a global city, a cultural capital, a symbol of Israel's modernity—was vulnerable, the pressure on Iron Dome grew exponentially. It rose to the challenge.

In May 2021 alone, over 4,300 rockets were fired into Israel. Iron Dome intercepted over 1,500 of them, most of them headed for population centres. In multiple videos shot by residents, one can see the night sky flash with streaks of light—Tamir missiles racing to meet their targets. Sometimes you hear cheers after a successful interception. Other times, just silence.

The system's performance became the face of Israel's resilience, not only militarily, but psychologically. It allowed daily life to resume minutes after an alert. It preserved national morale. And it did so without resorting to escalation or retaliation as the only answer. In a region where conflict is often defined by blood and vengeance, Iron Dome became something rare: a defensive victory.

◆◆◆

Around the world, Iron Dome captured imaginations. It featured in think-tank panels, military expos, and congressional briefings. Analysts praised its real-world effectiveness, not just lab-tested claims. The U.S. funded parts of its development and even purchased two batteries for its own use.

South Korea, facing artillery threats from the North, studied it. India discussed integrating it with its own systems. Azerbaijan deployed a version of it during its war with Armenia.

What made it exceptional was not just technology, but timing: Iron Dome was the first missile defence system to become a household name.

It inspired civilian confidence in a way few military assets do. People believed in it. They trusted it. That emotional buy-in is often missing in warfighting tools. But Iron Dome stood above a deeper truth: defence can also be a form of deterrence.

If you can deny the attacker success—not always by attacking back, but by denying the damage itself—you change the rules of the game.

◆◆◆

Iron Dome isn't perfect. No system is. In May 2021, a few rockets did get through, overwhelming the system's finite interceptor stock and revealing that even a 90% success rate leaves room for tragedy.

Critics point to the cost imbalance: a $500 rocket vs a $100,000 interceptor. Over time, this math becomes politically unsustainable.

Israel is already working on solutions: Iron Beam, a laser-based system that can destroy drones and rockets using energy rather than explosives, at a fraction of the cost per shot. In the meantime, Iron Dome remains the guardian on the wall—still deployed, still intercepting, still evolving.

◆◆◆

What Iron Dome represents is more than tactical ingenuity. It represents a shift in how we think about power.

In most histories, heroism is reactive. A retaliatory strike. A bold advance. But in Iron Dome's story, heroism is preventive. The missiles it destroys save lives we never get to mourn, homes we never have to rebuild, and wars that never escalate.

CHAPTER 27

◆◆◆

Interlude IV: Starlink and the Sky Over Ukraine

Elon Musk's Starlink project has been pivotal to Ukraine's air defence, communications, and electronic warfare in its war with Russia—and a civilian-owned satellite constellation became a strategic asset in modern war.

When Russia launched its full-scale invasion of Ukraine on 24 February 2022, one of its earliest and least visible moves was a massive cyber and electronic warfare assault on Ukrainian communications. Key military radio towers, satellite networks, and even parts of the Viasat satellite internet infrastructure were knocked offline.

Command chains faltered. Units on the front lost contact with headquarters. Air defence radars in some areas were temporarily blinded by EW attacks. A war that had begun with missiles was now being fought through silence.

And then, Starlink came online.

What Is Starlink?

Starlink is a satellite internet constellation project developed by SpaceX, the aerospace company founded by Elon Musk. Unlike traditional satellite internet systems that rely on a few geostationary satellites orbiting ~36,000 kilometres above Earth, Starlink operates thousands of low Earth orbit (LEO) satellites at altitudes between 340 and 1,200 kilometres.

The advantages:

Low latency: Data travels faster, critical for military operations.

High coverage: Can serve rural and frontline areas unreachable by fibre or cell networks.

Quick deployment: Requires only a compact user terminal ("Dishy McFlatface") and power.

Hard to jam: Signals bounce between many satellites, and directional antennas make them difficult targets.

By early 2022, over 2,000 Starlink satellites were already in orbit.

A Civilian Network Becomes a Strategic Asset

At Ukraine's request, Elon Musk directed SpaceX to activate Starlink service over Ukraine within days of the invasion. Terminals were shipped rapidly—some funded by SpaceX, others by Western allies.

What started as a backup internet option quickly became a lifeline for military command, civilian government, and resistance forces.

Ukrainian units began coordinating drone strikes using Starlink uplinks, linking radar and counter-UAS systems through Starlink when terrestrial lines were jammed, streaming real-time video feeds from loitering munitions to command posts, and maintaining encrypted communication for command and control even under heavy cyber attack.

Starlink doesn't shoot down missiles, but it enables those who do. In Ukraine's fragmented battlespace, Starlink has become the nervous system for short-range air defence (SHORAD) units, especially those defending mobile or urban sites.

Drone-spotting squads relay live feeds to ZSU-23-4 Shilka and Gepard gun operators, cueing them to engage UAVs before visual contact.

MANPADS teams receive alerts from drones scanning the horizon, allowing faster orientation and target acquisition.

Starlink terminals are even mounted on vehicles and field radars, keeping them connected to AD command hubs while constantly on the move.

In an environment where ground-based radar jamming is routine, Starlink has become the skybridge over the silence.

Inside the Ukranian Battlespace (Courtesy: New York Times)

The Russian Response: Target the Signal

Russia was quick to realise the military advantage Starlink conferred. According to reports, Russian EW units attempted to jam Starlink terminals, especially near the frontlines. In some cases, GPS spoofing was used to make terminals miscalculate their location. There were even fears of kinetic strikes on identified Starlink ground terminals, forcing Ukrainian teams to keep them mobile and well-camouflaged.

However, Starlink adapted by updating its firmware to increase resistance to jamming. Frequency hopping protocols were introduced. Musk personally acknowledged deploying anti-jamming updates "faster than the adversary could adapt."

Ethical and Strategic Dilemmas

While Starlink's role was widely praised, it also raised uncomfortable questions.

Should a private tech billionaire have the power to turn off or deny battlefield connectivity? Who ensures continuity of service if political tensions arise? What if Starlink becomes a target in space—do adversaries then target satellites?

In October 2022, Elon Musk reportedly limited Starlink's coverage in Crimea, citing the desire to avoid escalation. This drew sharp criticism from Ukrainian officials and highlighted the fragile, privately held nature of an asset being used for national defence.

The Broader Impact: A Blueprint for Others

Starlink's use in Ukraine has transformed military thinking worldwide. Key takeaways for air defence:

Future AD systems must integrate with commercial satellite constellations for redundancy.

Militaries are now considering leasing LEO satellite capacity during wartime.

SpaceX's success has accelerated similar projects, like OneWeb (UK-India), Kuiper (Amazon), and China's Guowang constellation.

For India, Starlink's Ukraine role has triggered debate about developing military-owned LEO constellations, fast-tracking Netra and GAGAN satellite upgrades, and integrating IACCS and DRDO assets with private space providers under strict regulation.

Starlink was never designed as a weapon. But in Ukraine, it has become one—not by destroying, but by enabling. In a war where the one who sees first often shoots first, Starlink made Ukraine's eyes faster and its arms longer.

The next great leap in air defence may not come from a new missile or radar. It may come from the shape of a satellite network, built in peacetime, weaponised in war.

CHAPTER 28

◆◆◆

Interlude V: India's Missile Man—Dr A.P.J. Abdul Kalam

He began his life on the edge of the Indian Ocean, the son of a boatman, in a house that smelled of salt and prayer. In the pre-dawn hours of Rameswaram, young Kalam sold newspapers before walking barefoot to school with a satchel of dreams. He wasn't born into privilege, but he was born with a mind that reached upward.

The sky fascinated him—not just as a dome above, but as a field of possibility. And decades later, he would make it India's first line of defence.

The Scientist Who Rewired National Pride

When Dr. A.P.J. Abdul Kalam joined the Defence Research and Development Organisation (DRDO) in the 1960s, India had barely begun to imagine building its own missile systems. We were dependent, sanctioned, and surrounded. But Kalam—quiet, wiry, and relentless—was already calculating escape velocity.

At ISRO, he helped design the SLV-3, India's first satellite launch vehicle, which lofted Rohini into orbit in 1980. But it was his return to DRDO in the early 1980s, handpicked by Prime Minister Indira Gandhi, that changed India's military sky forever.

There, he was made head of the Integrated Guided Missile Development Programme (IGMDP)—an ambitious five-missile roadmap that would give India:

Prithvi (earth) – for battlefield dominance

Trishul (trident) – for quick-reaction air defence

Akash (sky) – a surface-to-air shield

Nag (cobra) – for anti-tank precision

And Agni (fire) – the long arm of nuclear deterrence

In under a decade, these missiles moved from theoretical sketches to test ranges, shaking the sands of Pokhran, Chandipur, and Wheeler Island.

◆◆◆

Among the five, Akash was closest to Kalam's air defence vision.

He believed that for a nation as vast and exposed as India, air defence must be indigenous, mobile, and multi-layered. Under his leadership, Akash was developed as a medium-range surface-to-air missile (SAM) capable of protecting mobile tank columns, air bases, and command posts.

It used a ramjet propulsion system—a rare feat at the time—giving it sustained speed and range.

Kalam advocated for a networked defence grid, long before India had IACCS, linking Akash with radars like Rajendra to create a responsive air shield.

Though delayed in deployment, Akash became the proof that India could design its own defensive sky without depending on Russian or Western imports.

Even decades later, Akash is still being upgraded and exported.

He Dared to Dream of the Unseen

Kalam was not just a scientist of hardware. He was a thinker of doctrines. He understood that air defence was not just about intercepting. It was about dissuading. A missile that could retaliate made you safer than one that could only defend, and India's strategic sky needed both a shield and a sword—and he helped build both.

He once said, "War is never good. But if it comes, the other side should know your sky is not empty."

From Missile Man to President

In 2002, India did something extraordinary. It chose a scientist, not a politician, as its President. Abdul Kalam was catapulted from missile silos to Rashtrapati Bhavan—and the people followed him with love.

He travelled constantly, meeting schoolchildren, answering letters, lecturing defence academies, and still advising scientists. Even in the final years of his presidency, he asked for updates on the Agni-V's canister launch tests, the BMD (Ballistic Missile Defence) shield prototypes, and the Akash missile's live deployment.

His was a mind that never disengaged.

◆◆◆

Dr Kalam passed away on stage while delivering a lecture on creating a liveable planet—still dreaming, still teaching. But his fingerprints are on everything that keeps India safe today:

On the Agni missile, which protects our borders.

On Akash, which watches our skies.

On India's missile-manufacturing ecosystem, now being exported to the Philippines, Vietnam, and beyond.

Even India's hypersonic glide vehicle and anti-satellite missile, tested after his passing, drew from the fire he lit.

Dr. A.P.J. Abdul Kalam never wore a uniform. But he built what uniforms now defend. He never waged war, but ensured India would never be easy to threaten.

He gave India not just weapons, but the courage to believe in its own engineering.

Not just deterrence, but dignity.

Not just air defence systems, but an air defence culture.

If the sky above India is today watched, shielded, and respected, it is in no small part because a boy from Rameswaram once dared to measure it in trajectories, not stars.

CHAPTER 29

◆◆◆

Interlude VI: BrahMos and the Doctrine of Precision

In the late 90s, India was a country still recovering from sanctions. The Pokhran-II nuclear tests had shaken the world's diplomatic table. The Kargil War would soon prove that high-altitude, high-precision warfare was no longer a fantasy, but a requirement.

The military had always wanted something bold—a missile that was fast, precise, and untouchable. Something that could hit a target in minutes, from a safe distance. Something that could penetrate defences and break nerve centres before a war even escalated.

Enter BrahMos.

The Fusion of Two Rivers

The name BrahMos itself is a portmanteau—Brahmaputra, symbolising India, and Moskva, representing Russia. The missile was born of a joint venture between India's DRDO and Russia's NPO Mashinostroyenia, signed in 1998.

At its core, BrahMos fused the Russian P-800 Oniks supersonic cruise missile platform with Indian targeting, command, and navigation systems, and indigenous components, materials, and software interfaces

From the start, BrahMos was intended not as a platform, but as a family of platforms:

Land-based mobile launchers

Ship-launched vertical cells

Submarine tubes

Air-launched versions

And possibly, in the future, hypersonic upgrades

What Makes BrahMos Different

BrahMos is a supersonic cruise missile, meaning it travels at Mach 2.8 to Mach 3.0—three times faster than the speed of sound. It can fly at low altitudes (10–15 metres) during the terminal phase and has a range of 300–500 kilometres (extended in newer versions). It uses active radar homing and inertial navigation, allowing pinpoint accuracy (CEP < 1 metre)

Unlike ballistic missiles, BrahMos follows a flatter, more unpredictable trajectory, making it harder for traditional air defences to intercept.

In testing, BrahMos has been observed skimming sea waves at Mach 2.8, performing S-manoeuvres just before impact, and striking moving naval targets with centimetre-level precision.

India's military treats BrahMos as both a tactical weapon and a strategic enabler. Its roles include:

Anti-Access/Area Denial (A2/AD)

Deployed along coastal and border regions, BrahMos batteries create kill zones where enemy ships or aircraft can't operate freely.

First-Strike on Enemy Command Posts

Its precision and speed allow it to destroy radar installations, missile batteries, C2 (Command and Control) bunkers, and logistics convoys, within 3 to 5 minutes of launch.

Surgical Precision Against High-Value Targets

During mobilisations post-Uri or Balakot, BrahMos was seen as the go-to option for destroying terror camps or military launch pads without escalating to full-blown war.

The Offensive Edge

It is used to pre-emptively strike enemy SAM systems before air superiority operations, neutralise AWACS bases, radar hubs, and AD nodes, and create corridors for Indian Air Force strikes, punching holes in enemy AD grids.

The IAF's Su-30MKI-BrahMos integration is especially potent. A single aircraft can launch BrahMos from 400+ kilometres outside AD range, turn back before entering the danger zone, and hit time-sensitive, well-defended targets in five–seven minutes.

◆◆◆

It is deployed on all fronts.

Land-Based Units are deployed in Arunachal Pradesh, Ladakh, Rajasthan, and Andhra coast, use high-mobility launchers with three-minute setup time, and are connected to satellite and ISR feeds for live targeting.

Naval Platforms where it is deployed include the Rajput, Talwar, and Visakhapatnam-class destroyers. It is fired in vertical launch mode, and can hit ships or coastal targets, allowing the Indian Navy to dominate littoral warfare and impose sea denial

The air-launched versions are integrated with Su-30MKI (under Project BrahMos-A). Successfully test-fired in 2017 and refined since then, it is a game-changer for quick-strike air operations against AD sites.

◆◆◆

BrahMos is now an export-ready system, with interest from the Philippines, which signed a $375 million deal for coastal defence batteries, along with Vietnam, Indonesia, and UAE (United Arab

Emirates), expressing strong interest, while South Africa and Brazil, are exploring ship-borne variants.

Exports of BrahMos send a signal: India is not just a user, but a strategic supplier of precision deterrence.

(Courtesy: Brahmos.com)

The BrahMos-II (K), a hypersonic variant expected to touch Mach 7 with the incorporation of scramjet technology will have a range extension to 1,000+ kilometres with lighter warheads, and AI-driven guidance for target discrimination in cluttered or urban zones. These advances will blur the line between tactical and strategic, allowing India to strike further, faster, and smarter, and deny airspace not just defensively, but by erasing the sensors that defend it.

◆◆◆

BrahMos is not just a missile. It is a doctrine in motion.

It represents speed as survival, precision as persuasion, and technology as deterrence.

In the layered latticework of air defence and offence, BrahMos is the hammer that clears the sky by striking the ground.

It does not shield. It disables the eyes that aim.

It does not wait. It breaks the rhythm of the enemy's plan.

It is not a warning. It is what follows the warning—too fast to stop.

CHAPTER 30

◆◆◆

Interlude VII: Agni and the Strategic Spine

The purpose of Agni is not war. It is memory. It reminds the world that India will never start a fire, but will never be consumed by one.

In 1983, under a veil of scientific ambition and strategic urgency, India launched the Integrated Guided Missile Development Programme (IGMDP). The five-pillar project—Prithvi, Trishul, Akash, Nag, and Agni—was not just about missiles. It was about sovereignty in the age of denial.

Sanctions loomed. Technology was blocked. And the Cold War's nuclear cloud cast long shadows over South Asia.

Of the five, Agni was the fire that mattered most.

Technology Demonstrator to Strategic Backbone

Originally tested in 1989 as a technology demonstrator, the first Agni missile was essentially an extended Prithvi SRBM with a second-stage solid motor. But even in this primitive form, it flew with purpose. It said, quietly but unmistakably, that India was entering the world of ballistic missiles.

The Agni programme was reclassified as a long-term strategic project in the 1990s, directly linked to the nation's minimum credible deterrence doctrine.

Today, Agni is not a missile. It is a family of missiles, ranging from medium- to intercontinental-range platforms.

The Arsenal of Agni

Agni-I

Range: ~700–900 kilometres
Role: Theatre deterrent, Pakistan-specific
Launch platform: Road-mobile TELs (Transporter Erector Launchers)

Agni-II

Range: ~2,000–2,500 kilometres
Reach: Pakistan and parts of western China
Deployed: With India's Strategic Forces Command (SFC)

Agni-III

Range: ~3,500–5,000 kilometres
Role: Credible second-strike against deep Chinese targets
Launched: From rail-mobile platforms for survivability

Agni-IV and V

Agni-IV (~4,000 kilometres): Precision intermediate-range
Agni-V (~5,000–5,500 kilometres): India's first canisterised intercontinental ballistic missile (ICBM), capable of targeting entire Asia and parts of Europe

Agni-P (Prime)

Latest entrant with composite motor casing, enhanced accuracy, and anti-BMD manoeuvres
Developed with Manoeuvrable Re-Entry Vehicle (MaRV) capability in mind

All Agni variants use solid fuel propulsion, allowing quicker launch and greater storage.

(Courtesy: Wikimedia Commons)

Deterrence, Not Deployment

India follows a doctrine of No First Use (NFU). The Agni series is therefore not an offensive tool, but a strategic deterrent—a reminder to potential adversaries that any nuclear aggression will be met with overwhelming retaliation.

Agni missiles are placed under the Strategic Forces Command (SFC) and are only launched with clearance from the Nuclear Command Authority, chaired by the Prime Minister. This civilian-led control and military professionalism make India's deterrent posture credible, restrained, and responsive.

How Agni Supports Air Defence

While Agni itself is not an air defence system, it is deeply intertwined with the logic of air defence.

Strategic deterrence creates air defence gaps. Knowing that India has long-range Agni missiles deters adversaries from launching massed nuclear strikes, reducing the need for high-volume interception.

Force Dispersion—Agni's mobility ensures survivability, meaning India does not rely solely on interception but on assured retaliation, forming the second tier of strategic air defence.

Credible Counterforce Option—Agni-P and Agni-V can hit enemy nuclear and air defence infrastructure in the opening moments of retaliation.

In simpler terms, air defence is the shield.

Agni is the certainty that a sword still lies behind it.

◆◆◆

Over the decades, Agni has been test-fired with increasing regularity, not just for validation, but to send signals:

During India-China tensions in Ladakh, Agni-III and Agni-V were test-fired within weeks, reminding Beijing of India's strategic depth.

Canisterised tests showed adversaries that missiles could be launched within minutes, with no detectable preparation.

MIRV (Multiple Independently Targetable Re-entry Vehicles) development was hinted at through Agni-V's upgrade cycle, subtly messaging the next leap in survivable deterrence.

Other Strategic Missiles

India possesses several other strategic missile systems beyond the Agni and BrahMos families—each designed for specific roles across the spectrum of deterrence, force projection, and survivable response. While Agni represents the long-range nuclear-capable backbone and BrahMos the precision, high-speed tactical edge, the others serve both niche strategic and escalatory thresholds.

Here's a consolidated view of India's strategic missile ecosystem beyond Agni and BrahMos:

Prithvi Series – The Theatre-Level Nuclear Option

Includes the Prithvi-I, II, III (Surface-to-surface short-range ballistic missiles)

Range: 150–350 kilometres

Payload: 500–1,000 kg
Propulsion: Liquid-fuel
Nuclear-capable: Yes
Role: Tactical deterrent against short-range targets in Pakistan and possibly Tibet.
Originally developed under the IGMDP, the Prithvi missiles are now mostly relegated to training roles or limited tactical reserve, as solid-fuel and longer-range systems like Agni and BrahMos become frontline assets.

Shaurya Missile – The Canisterised Cold Fire

Range: ~700–1,900 kilometres
Type: Hypersonic quasi-ballistic missile
Launch: Canisterised, from underground silos or mobile platforms
Speed: Mach 7+
Nuclear-capable: Yes
Shaurya is believed to be the land-based version of the K-15 Sagarika SLBM, offering India a second-strike option that is hard to track, easy to store, and very fast.
Its hypersonic speed and depressed trajectory make it difficult to intercept by conventional air defence systems.

K Series (Submarine-Launched Ballistic Missiles) – India's Undersea Firepower

K-15 (Sagarika)
Range: 750–1,000 kilometres
Platform: Arihant-class SSBN
Nuclear-capable: Yes
Status: Operational

K-4
Range: 3,500 kilometres
Status: Under testing
Will allow Indian SSBNs to strike deeper inland from sea, particularly targeting China's interior.

K-5 and K-6 (Reportedly under development)

With MIRV capability and ranges exceeding 5,000 kilometres

The K series is vital for India's nuclear triad, ensuring second-strike credibility from undersea platforms—making any attack survivable and retaliation inevitable.

Nirbhay Cruise Missile – The Long Arm of Precision

Type: Subsonic, terrain-hugging cruise missile
Range: ~1,000 kilometres
Launch: Ground/air/ship-based
Warhead: Conventional and nuclear variants possible
Navigation: Indigenous Ring Laser Gyro + GPS/GLONASS/NavIC
Status: In limited series production
Nirbhay is India's equivalent of the U.S. Tomahawk, offering deep strike options in contested airspaces with very low radar signature, especially relevant in suppression of enemy air defence (SEAD) missions.

Surya ICBM (Unconfirmed/Rumoured) – India's Potential Intercontinental Reach

Rumoured Range: 8,000–12,000 kilometres
Status: Not officially acknowledged
Believed to be an Agni-VI variant with MIRV capability
Surya may eventually allow India to project deterrence globally, especially against faraway nuclear powers.

Anti-Satellite (ASAT) Missile – Strategic Denial in Space

Mission Shakti test in 2019 proved India's kinetic ASAT capability
Missile derived from modified Prithvi Defence Vehicle (PDV) interceptor
Not for regular use, but provides space deterrence—denying adversaries access to orbital intelligence or communication
While not a strategic nuclear weapon, it's a strategic enabler—capable of crippling command and surveillance infrastructure in early stages of war.

The Agni missile series is as much a diplomatic tool as a military one.

It allows India to assert itself as a responsible nuclear state with full-spectrum capability, balance regional equations without needing forward-deployed nuclear assets, and signal strategic autonomy from both Western and Eastern alliances.

India has repeatedly clarified that Agni is for deterrence, not aggression. But its very presence influences adversary planning, reshapes air defence doctrines, and forces caution into every pre-war calculation.

Reports suggest the development of Agni-VI with a range up to 10,000 kilometres, with MIRV or MaRV capabilities, and the Agni Hypersonic Glide Vehicle (HGV) variants. Integration of AI for mid-course correction, space-based launch control, and anti-BMD evasion is also under way.

When these arrive, Agni will become more than a retaliatory instrument. It will be a strategic signal in flight, unseen until it's too late to stop.

Agni is not fired in war.

It is deployed in doctrine, speech, and silence.

It lies in wait not to launch first but to ensure there is no need to launch at all.

CHAPTER 31

◆◆◆

Interlude VIII: When Underdogs Win—The Paradox of Asymmetric Air Warfare

Insurgents with shoulder-fired weapons and low-tech tactics have repeatedly challenged and sometimes thwarted the air supremacy of great powers—from Afghanistan to Yemen.

The 20th and 21st centuries were meant to belong to air power. From the flash of Hiroshima to the shock and awe of Baghdad, the aircraft—be it bomber, drone, or gunship—became the modern symbol of military dominance. For the great powers, it was not just a weapon—it was a promise: that no matter how far or remote, control of the sky meant control of the ground.

And yet, time and again, that promise met its match in the mountains, jungles, and alleys where conventional doctrine faltered, and a different kind of war was being fought.

The sky, it turned out, was never as invincible as it looked from above.

Stingers Turn of the Tide

In the 1980s, the Soviet Union brought to Afghanistan a devastating aerial arsenal. Mi-24 Hind gunships, MiG fighters, and heavy bombers rained fire on Mujahideen positions, often turning villages into rubble before ground troops ever arrived. But in 1986, a single weapon shifted the balance: the FIM-92 Stinger.

Provided covertly by the United States, the Stinger was a shoulder-fired infrared missile that locked onto the heat signature of aircraft. In the hands of an untrained fighter, it turned the air war upside down. Suddenly, Soviet pilots began to fear low-altitude runs. Gunships flew higher. Supply lines became vulnerable. The sky was no longer theirs.

By 1989, the Soviets had withdrawn. The war was lost. And the image that lingered wasn't a tank, but a bearded man with a launcher slung across his back, scanning the heavens.

The Stinger being used in Afghanistan (Courtesy: Internet Archive)

The Americans in Afghanistan and Iraq – Deja Vu

When the United States returned to Afghanistan after 9/11, it came with greater firepower and better precision. Drones loitered for hours. B-52s dropped JDAMs (Joint Direct Attack Munitions) with satellite accuracy. And yet, slowly and inexorably, the sky began to feel smaller.

In narrow valleys and rugged terrain, MANPADS (Man-Portable Air Defence Systems)—older variants like SA-7s and newer black-market versions—began to reappear. In Iraq, too, insurgents used quadruple-A (anti-aircraft artillery), heat-seeking weapons, and timed RPG (Rocket-Propelled Grenade) strikes to harass and occasionally bring down helicopters. The iconic Black Hawk Down wasn't just a metaphor. It was a reality repeated in Tikrit, Fallujah, and Helmand.

The insurgents had no air force. But they didn't need one. Their strategy was simple: deny the enemy the confidence to fly low, to fly close, to fly often.

Vietnam – The Jungle That Bit Back

Long before the mountains of Afghanistan, it was the jungles of Vietnam that first taught the Americans this lesson. There, the North Vietnamese Army and Viet Cong used a lethal mix of Soviet-supplied SAMs, AAA batteries, and small arms fire to turn the skies into a killing field. More than 10,000 U.S. aircraft were lost in Vietnam, not from dogfights—but from terrain-embedded, ground-fired, low-tech threats.

Airfields were ambushed. Runways were shelled. Gunships were grounded. In a war where the U.S. expected to dominate from above, it was again the ground that dictated the terms of fear.

The Houthis and the Modern Playbook

In Yemen, the Houthi rebels—vastly outgunned and out-teched—have repeatedly struck Saudi and Emirati aircraft using Iranian-supplied MANPADS and, increasingly, surface-to-air missiles adapted from other platforms. In some cases, they've shot down U.S.-made drones. In others, they've forced commercial traffic to reroute.

Even more remarkably, they have done this while being constantly surveilled and targeted by some of the most advanced ISR (intelligence, surveillance, and reconnaissance) systems in the world.

The message is clear: air power is only as dominant as the cost it doesn't incur. Once insurgents begin to raise that cost—whether in equipment, pilot lives, or psychological confidence—the sky begins to shrink.

The Paradox of Air Supremacy

These stories reveal a military paradox: air superiority is both an overwhelming advantage and a fragile illusion. It is effective when the adversary is exposed, static, and lacks cover. But insurgents do not play by those rules. They hide. They move. They blend. And when they shoot, they often shoot from ambush, with patience, not pursuit.

Moreover, for the great powers, every aircraft downed is a political and moral shockwave. The loss of a pilot, a downed helicopter, a captured drone—these are not just tactical setbacks. They are symbols. And insurgents, for all their crude weapons, understand symbols well.

What does this mean for the defenders?

It means that air defence must not only look up—but also down. It must map heat signatures of hidden launchers, predict guerrilla ambushes, suppress radar-less threats, and track portable systems in hands as mobile as they are invisible. It must train for incomplete airspace, where superiority is conditional, not assumed.

◆◆◆

Operation Sindoor offered a taste of this challenge. Small, agile UAVs. Makeshift jammers. Decoys and dummy targets. And in the future, it will get murkier still: loitering munitions launched from pickup trucks, home-modified drones, civilian infrastructure weaponised in plain sight.

Air power is still decisive. But it is no longer unchallenged. And the lesson from every mountain and alley is simple: the sky does not belong to those who fly it, but to those who can deny it.

CHAPTER 32

◆◆◆

Interlude IX: The Watershed Moment in Air Defence—9/11

Until the morning of 11 September 2001, air defence meant looking outward. The assumption—the doctrine—was that threats came from outside. From rival nations. From identified flight paths. From visible signatures.

But at 8.46 AM, when American Airlines Flight 11 crashed into the North Tower of the World Trade Center, and again at 9.03 AM, when United Airlines Flight 175 struck the South Tower, the very geometry of threat collapsed. The sky itself had been turned inward.

Commercial aircraft—symbols of civilian mobility, icons of globalisation—had been weaponised not by technology, but by intent. The passengers were real. The planes were scheduled. The transponders were familiar. The routes were routine. But the minds inside the cockpit were no longer flying toward a destination. They were flying toward an idea—to hijack not just aircraft, but imagination.

The United States, with its trillion-dollar defence infrastructure, its vaunted NORAD command, its unmatched interceptor fleet and satellite constellations, was caught in a silence of the wrong kind. The radars were on. The planes were tracked. But the system was not trained to disbelieve its own airspace.

It was the perfect bypass of doctrine. No transnational air defence shield had been designed for the idea that an airliner, full of citizens, could be steered like a missile. The enemy had not broken through the radar. It had ridden inside it.

◆◆◆

Within minutes, the attack became more than symbolic. The Pentagon itself—the epicentre of military planning—was struck. A fourth aircraft, United 93, was heading toward either the Capitol or the White House before passengers heroically intervened, bringing it down in a field in Pennsylvania.

The Pentagon after it was hit
(Courtesy: Wikipedia)

In that one morning, the concept of air defence had been rendered obsolete, not in technology, but in theory. The world saw not just steel fall, but certainty. That airspace could be managed. That threats would look like threats. That security could be codified.

After 9/11, those illusions died alongside the thousands who perished.

Rethinking the Shield

In the aftermath, the United States rewrote its air defence philosophy almost overnight. NORAD, long tasked with tracking threats coming from beyond the oceans, now turned its gaze inward. A new concept emerged: domestic air defence of civil aviation, a contradiction in terms just days before.

Fighter jets were now tasked with shadowing suspicious aircraft within their own airspace. Pilots were trained for scenarios where they might have to shoot down hijacked commercial planes, possibly with civilians onboard, to prevent a greater catastrophe. The moral calculus of war had entered the homeland, and it wore the clothes of peace.

Air marshals were introduced. Cockpit doors were reinforced. Ground radar networks were integrated with counterterrorism databases. The Federal Aviation Administration (FAA) began liaising with the military in real-time. Air defence became not just kinetic—it became bureaucratic, digital, and psychological.

◆◆◆

Across the world, countries watched and learned. India, which had already faced the 1999 Kandahar hijacking, now reconsidered how rogue aviation could be part of a future enemy playbook. New radar networks were commissioned. No-fly zones over cities became more aggressively patrolled. The IAF's peacetime alert posture was re-examined.

Civilian air traffic control systems were hardened. Exercises began including scenarios with hijacked aircraft, stray drones, radio-silent planes, and even friendly-fire protocols.

Because 9/11 had proven something devastatingly simple: even the strongest shield is useless if it is facing the wrong way.

◆◆◆

The genius of 9/11 lay not in new weapons, but in the inversion of trust. Passengers trusted pilots. Towers trusted aircraft. Systems trusted procedures. In hijacking commercial planes, the attackers had not just flown into buildings—they had flown into the blind spots of civilisation.

Air defence had always been trained to recognise the "other."

9/11 demanded that it recognise the "familiar" gone rogue.

This was a shift of enormous consequence. It meant air defence could no longer be a martial function alone—it had to become a psychological discipline, a societal posture, a doctrine that included civilians, controllers, cockpit crews, intelligence analysts, and airport staff.

The enemy had walked through the terminal, not launched from a silo.

◆◆◆

Since 9/11, the U.S. and its allies have thwarted dozens of attempted airborne threats—some from drones, some from chartered flights, some from within their own systems. Many will never be publicly known. But what changed that day is permanent: air defence is no longer just military. It is homeland. It is civilian. It is institutional.

And it is eternally paranoid, by design.

In a strange way, 9/11 brought air defence closer to the ground—not in altitude, but in urgency and intimacy. The sky, once sacred, now needed to be distrusted.

And that may be the greatest shift of all. Not in radar range, or missile speed, or interception geometry—but in the human relationship with the sky itself.

PART III

◆◆◆

INDIA'S AIR DEFENCE

What is the military history of India's Air Defence since WWII? How was the Corps of AAD formed? How have we fared till *Op Sindoor*? UNFOLD the answers in this part.

CHAPTER 33

◆◆◆

Air Defence in British India and the Crucible of World War II (1939–1947)

The establishment of Air Defence Artillery in India was not born of long-term strategic planning, but a direct and urgent response to the outbreak of the Second World War in 1939.

The aerial threat posed by the rapid advances of the Japanese military in East Asia compelled the British to address the vulnerability of their Indian territories.

The initial focus was modest—train a small contingent of Indian troops in the operation of basic anti-aircraft artillery, a skill set that was rapidly becoming indispensable on battlefields across the globe.

But the bravery of men like Havildar Sham Lal and Gunner Balbir Singh, the first Indian anti-aircraft gunners to be honoured with the Indian Distinguished Service Medal for their gallantry under fire, laid the foundations of valour and sacrifice on which the edifice of India's modern air defence was built.

Pioneering Units and Early Equipment

In September 1940, the first anti-aircraft training battery began its formation in Colaba, Mumbai. This initiative quickly expanded, with the Number 1 Anti-Aircraft Training Centre commencing its raising in Colaba and completing its establishment in Karachi by

January 1941. The choice of these coastal cities, one on the west coast and the other strategically positioned in what would later become Pakistan, underscored the maritime and overland threat perceptions of the time.

The initial arsenal of these fledgling units consisted primarily of 3-inch "Ack-Ack" guns. These were soon supplemented by the more versatile and effective Bofors 40mm L/60 light anti-aircraft guns, a weapon system that would achieve legendary status during the war and continue in service for decades thereafter. The crucial role of experienced cadres in jump-starting this new arm is evident in the involvement of the 8th Heavy Anti-Aircraft (HAA) Battery of the Royal Artillery, which provided not only some of the initial equipment but also the training expertise necessary to build proficiency among the Indian recruits.

From these training establishments emerged the first dedicated Indian anti-aircraft units. The Royal High Altitude Airship ("R" HAA) Regiment, later known as the 1st Indian HAA Regiment, was formed at Colaba, its nucleus drawn from the No. 1 Indian Anti-Aircraft Technical Training Battery. Close on its heels, in January 1941, the "U" Anti-Aircraft Regiment (later 1st Indian Light Anti-Aircraft Regiment) was raised at Malir Cantonment, near Karachi. These pioneering regiments, equipped with a mix of HAA and LAA (Light Anti-Aircraft) guns, represented India's first organised response to the challenge of air defence.

The Malayan Campaign and the Gallantry of the 1st Indian HAA Regiment

The story of the 1st Indian Heavy Anti-Aircraft Regiment is one of both heroism and tragedy. Even before its formation was complete, the No. 1 HAA Battery of the regiment was dispatched to the remote oilfields of Digboi in Assam, a vital resource that needed protection from potential Japanese air raids.

The remainder of the regiment, augmented by the 1st and 5th Light Anti-Aircraft (LAA) Batteries, embarked on a fateful journey in August 1941, sailing to Singapore as part of a desperate attempt to bolster the British Malaya Command's defences against the anticipated Japanese onslaught. Upon arrival, this unusually large formation, comprising 1,250 Other Ranks and 111 Followers, officered by a mere 12 British officers of the Royal Artillery and nine Viceroy's Commissioned Officers (VCOs), was tasked with the air defence of critical installations across Singapore Island. These included the strategic airbases at Tengah and Seletar, the Naval Base East, and key supply depots.

As the Japanese invasion of Malaya unfolded and Singapore came under direct air attack, the gunners and their attached LAA batteries found themselves in the thick of the action. It was here, amidst the smoke and fire of battle, that the first Indian anti-aircraft gunners earned recognition for their bravery. Havildar Sham Lal and Gunner Balbir Singh, while manning their guns at Tengah airbase, displayed conspicuous gallantry under Japanese bombing and strafing. For their actions, they were awarded the Indian Distinguished Service Medal (IDSM), becoming the first of their kind to receive this honour. Their Commanding Officer, Lieutenant Colonel John Rowley Williamson, also demonstrated outstanding leadership in the face of overwhelming odds and was awarded the Distinguished Service Order (DSO), the only officer of the Indian Anti-Aircraft Artillery to be so decorated during the entire Second World War. Another officer, Lieutenant John A. Hopson, earned a Military Cross for his actions.

Despite these acts of individual and collective bravery, the Japanese forces, with superior numbers, air power, and a well-executed strategy, overwhelmed the Allied defences. On 15 February 1942, Singapore, the much-vaunted "Gibraltar of the East," fell. The 1st Indian HAA Regiment was among the Allied units that surrendered that day. The aftermath was grim for its personnel. Over 320 gunners of the regiment were killed in action or died later in the brutal conditions of Japanese captivity, transported on infamous "hell ships" to various parts of Asia. The regiment itself was never re-raised, and its story become a tragic testament to the sacrifices made.

Only a memorial in Singapore bears silent witness to the valour of these early Indian air defenders. This episode, blending heroism with ultimate loss, provides a powerful narrative thread in the early history of Indian air defence.

Defending the Homeland: The Japanese Air Raids on Calcutta and the AA Response

The war soon reached the shores of India. Calcutta (now Kolkata), then the capital of British India and a major port and industrial hub, became a prime target for the Imperial Japanese Army Air Force. From December 1942 through mid-1944, the city endured a series of air raids aimed at disrupting its port facilities, crippling war industries, and hampering Allied preparations for a counter-offensive in Burma.

The initial Japanese raids, commencing on 20 December 1942, caused significant damage to infrastructure and resulted in civilian casualties, leading to the displacement of an estimated 350,000 people from the city. However, Calcutta was not defenceless. Contemporary accounts suggest the city possessed "good air defence systems." These defences, primarily comprising anti-aircraft guns, reportedly forced Japanese bombers to fly at high altitudes, particularly during daylight, leading to many raids being conducted under the cover of darkness to minimise exposure to AA fire.

The responsibility for coordinating the air defence of this vital region fell to formations like the 2nd Indian Anti-Aircraft Brigade. Formed around May 1942 under the command of Brigadier (later Temporary Brigadier) Henry Herbert Montague Oliver, this brigade was specifically tasked with the protection of Calcutta and the numerous airfields in the Bengal area that were critical for Allied air operations. Its order of battle included Indian Heavy Anti-Aircraft (HAA) and Light Anti-Aircraft (LAA) regiments, such as the 3rd Indian HAA Regiment and the 2nd Indian LAA Regiment, alongside Royal Artillery units, reflecting the combined nature of the defence effort.

As the bombing campaign continued into 1943, the air defences of Calcutta were progressively strengthened. A significant development was the deployment of RADAR-guided night fighters by the Royal Air Force (RAF). These aircraft proved effective in intercepting Japanese bombers, with several Mitsubishi Ki-21 "Sally" and Mitsubishi Ki-46 "Dinah" reconnaissance bombers being shot down. This marked an important technological advancement, playing a direct role in the air defence of India, moving beyond purely gun-based systems to integrated fighter-radar operations.

However, the air defence shield was not impenetrable. A particularly devastating daylight raid occurred on 5 December 1943, when Japanese aircraft targeted Calcutta's Kidderpore Docks. The attack, reportedly meeting no resistance, caused hundreds of deaths and destroyed several ships and warehouses.

Expansion and Adaptation: Growth of AA Units, AA/ Atk Regiments, and the Burma Campaign

The escalating threat perception, particularly from the Japanese in the eastern theatre, spurred a considerable expansion of India's air defence capabilities throughout the war. By 1942, the air defence branch had grown to include eighteen operational anti-aircraft regiments—nine HAA and nine LAA—in addition to four dedicated AD brigades and some independent HAA and LAA batteries. This rapid growth continued, and by the end of 1944, the total number of air defence artillery units had reached thirty-three. This quantitative expansion was a clear indication of the lessons being learned about the importance of air defence in modern total war.

A noteworthy organisational adaptation during this period was the development of multi-role Anti-Aircraft/Anti-Tank (AA/Atk) regiments. This innovation was driven by the unique demands of the war against Japan in the India-Burma theatre. The difficult terrain of regions like Arakan and the Indo-Burmese border, coupled with the need for economy of resources and tactical flexibility, led to the concept of combining anti-aircraft and anti-tank capabilities within a single regimental structure. These regiments were typically envisioned to comprise two anti-tank batteries equipped with 6-pounder anti-tank guns and two anti-aircraft batteries, initially armed with twelve Bofors 40mm LAA guns, with an eventual plan to re-equip them with eighteen 20mm Hispano guns, which were effective in both anti-aircraft and ground roles.

The creation of Indian AA/Atk regiments, such as the 1st, 2nd, and 7th AA/Atk Regiments, I.A., proceeded, although often more slowly and erratically than their British counterparts, partly due to equipment availability.

The 26th Air Defence Regiment, which was originally raised as the 2nd Indian Light Anti-Aircraft Regiment in October 1941, saw extensive service in Bengal and Assam. It holds the distinction of being the only Air Defence Regiment to enter Rangoon with General Slim's XIV Army after its capture, highlighting its continuous involvement in the Burma Campaign.

The Legacy of Partition: Division of Assets and the Foundation for Independent India's AD

The end of World War II in 1945 brought about a significant demobilisation across the British Indian Army, and the newly expanded Air Defence branch was no exception. Many of the recently raised AA units were disbanded as the immediate wartime threat receded. This was a common pattern in post-war military establishments globally, but for India, it was compounded by the monumental political upheaval of the Partition in 1947.

The division of British India into independent India and Pakistan had profound consequences for the Armed Forces, including the Air Defence Artillery. Assets, units, and personnel were divided between the two new nations. Of the Air Defence units that remained, India retained only two Light Anti-Aircraft Regiments: the 26th LAA Regiment and the 27th LAA Regiment. This represented a stark reduction from the thirty-three AD artillery units that existed at the height of the war in 1944.

Crucially, the two oldest and arguably most experienced units, the I Training Battery and the "R" HAA Regiment (the erstwhile 1st Indian HAA Regiment that had fought in Malaya and Singapore), were transferred to Pakistan. This meant that independent India began its journey with a significantly diminished cadre of experienced AD personnel and a much-reduced number of established units. The institutional memory and combat experience embodied in units like the 1st Indian HAA Regiment were largely lost to India, creating a critical capability gap at a time when the new nation faced immediate and complex security challenges.

The 26th LAA Regiment, originally raised as the 2nd Indian LAA Regiment on 1 October 1941, and the 27th LAA Regiment, raised as the 3rd Indian LAA Regiment on 1 February 1942, formed the bedrock of India's post-independence Air Defence Artillery. These two regiments, with their wartime lineage, provided a thread of continuity and a foundation upon which the future Corps of Army Air Defence would eventually be built. However, the task of rebuilding and expanding from this small base, while simultaneously developing indigenous expertise and doctrine, would be a formidable challenge for the newly independent nation.

CHAPTER 34

◆◆◆

Guarding a New Nation—Air Defence in Independent India (1947–1970)

The 1947–48 Kashmir War

The ink had barely dried on the documents of India's independence when the nation was thrust into its first conflict: the 1947–48 war in Jammu and Kashmir. This war immediately underscored the importance of air power and, consequently, the necessity of air defence, however nascent its capabilities were at the time. The Royal Indian Air Force (RIAF) played a pivotal role from the outset, most dramatically in the airlift of troops from the 1st Battalion, The Sikh Regiment, to Srinagar on 27 October 1947. These forces arrived just in time to secure the vital Srinagar airfield from advancing Pakistani tribal lashkars and regular forces, an action widely credited with saving the Kashmir Valley for India.

In this context, the primary role of India's fledgling Air Defence Artillery was the protection of these critical airheads, which served as the lifelines for troops and supplies into the contested region. The 26 Light Anti-Aircraft (LAA) Regiment, one of the two LAA regiments retained by India after partition, was quickly called upon. In June 1948, one LAA Battery from this regiment, then stationed at Uruli, was moved to Jammu & Kashmir. Its troops were deployed to provide anti-aircraft cover for the Srinagar and Jammu airfields.

This deployment was a direct result of a directive from the Defence Committee of the Cabinet (DCC), highlighting the strategic importance attached to these airfields.

Simultaneously, new raisings were underway to bolster AD capabilities. The 19 Heavy Anti-Aircraft (HAA) Regiment was raised in April 1948, equipped with World War II-vintage 3.7-inch HAA guns. One battery from this newly raised regiment was deployed to protect the Pathankot airfield, another key staging point for operations in Kashmir.

The air threat from Pakistan during this conflict was limited, as the Royal Pakistan Air Force (RPAF) itself was in its infancy and did not undertake significant offensive missions against Indian forces in Kashmir. Pakistan deployed detachments of its 5th and 6th AA Regiments, and their guns were sometimes used in a ground role. However, RIAF aircraft operating in support of Indian ground troops regularly faced hostile ground fire. This often came from small arms, but Pakistani artillery also employed its mountain guns in an improvised anti-aircraft role, firing air-burst shells, notably in the Poonch sector. This environment, while not characterised by sophisticated enemy air attacks, still posed a tangible threat to low-flying RIAF aircraft engaged in reconnaissance and close support missions.

In March 1948, Flying Officer Balwant Singh, flying a Tempest fighter on a close support mission in the Naushera-Jhangar area, was hit by ground fire. His aircraft crashed, and he was killed, underscoring the dangers faced by aircrew even in the absence of a formidable enemy air force or sophisticated AD systems.

◆◆◆

The immediate aftermath of partition presented India's Air Defence arm with formidable challenges. The primary equipment available consisted mainly of World War II-vintage systems: the reliable Bofors 40mm L/60 guns, which had proven their worth globally, and some 3.7-inch HAA guns. Modernisation was a distant prospect; the immediate priority was consolidation and rebuilding a coherent AD structure from the limited resources at hand.

A critical step was the re-establishment of training infrastructure. The anti-aircraft training school that had been located in Karachi (now in Pakistan) was moved to India and merged into the air defence wing of the School of Artillery at Deolali. This became the primary institution for imparting AD training to Indian Army personnel in the early post-independence years.

Radar capabilities, a cornerstone of effective air defence, were particularly rudimentary. The No. 1 Radar Unit was made operational at Palam (Delhi) in 1948, equipped with a British Type 11 search radar (operating in the S-band, then referred to as 500 m/c band) and a Type 13 height-finding radar (operating in the 10 cm band). This marked the humble beginnings of India's independent radar network.

The 1962 Sino-Indian War

The 1962 Sino-Indian War was a watershed moment for the Indian military, delivering a traumatic shock and exposing critical deficiencies across the board. While the Indian Air Force (IAF) was, by some accounts, qualitatively superior to its Chinese counterpart at the time, a political decision was made not to employ it in an offensive combat role.

The war laid bare India's lack of preparedness for a conflict of that scale and nature. Shortages were rampant: from basic infantry weapons like modern rifles to essential logistical support like radio sets, field cables, and transport vehicles. Higher command structures and strategic planning were also found wanting.

From an air defence perspective, the 1962 conflict highlighted significant vulnerabilities. The existing radar cover was sparse and technologically dated. In 1962, the IAF's radar inventory included only one Type 8 radar, six Type 13 radars, and seven Type 14 and Type 15 radars. The operational effectiveness of these systems was severely hampered by ground clutter in the mountainous terrain and unreliable height information, degrading their ability to provide accurate early warning or effective fighter control. The deployment of these radars was primarily concentrated around major cities like Delhi, Calcutta, and Bombay, and a few Sector Operations Centres (SOCs) in the western sector, leaving vast swathes of the northern border inadequately covered.

Army AD units, such as the 26 Air Defence Regiment, were deployed in the Eastern Theatre during the conflict. In addition to their primary AD role, some detachments of the regiment were even employed in an infantry capacity in areas like Tawang and Senge in Arunachal Pradesh (then NEFA), reflecting the desperate situation on the ground.

The most profound lesson from the 1962 debacle for air defence was the stark realisation of its importance, even if air power was not fully committed. It became evident that if India were to leverage its air assets effectively in future conflicts, robust and modern air defence for its airbases, vital areas, and forward-deployed troops would be an absolute necessity.

The 1965 Indo-Pak War

The 1965 Indo-Pak War saw a significant escalation in air activity compared to previous conflicts, with both air forces actively engaging each other and ground targets. In this environment, India's Air Defence Artillery, though still primarily gun-based, played a crucial and often unsung role in the overall war effort. The performance of AD units during this conflict provided a vital validation of their utility and highlighted the courage and skill of their personnel.

Indian AD units were officially credited with shooting down 25 Pakistan Air Force (PAF) aircraft during the war. This was a substantial contribution to the air war, demonstrating the effectiveness of Indian gunners and their equipment against hostile aircraft. Conversely, Pakistani Anti-Aircraft Artillery (AAA) was responsible for downing 10 IAF aircraft, indicating that ground-based air defences were a significant factor for both sides. These figures underscore the intensity of ground-to-air engagements and the critical role AD played in the attrition of air assets.

One of the most notable anecdotes of individual bravery comes from the actions of Havildar Athanikal Basil Jesudasan of the 45 Air Defence Regiment. On 7 September 1965, his unit was deployed for the defence of an important air force installation in Amritsar, a key forward airbase. During an enemy air attack, Havildar Jesudasan displayed exceptional courage and skill, engaging a Pakistani F-86 Sabrejet with his anti-aircraft gun. He successfully damaged the enemy aircraft, forcing it to break off its attack and thereby saving the vital air force installation from potential destruction. For this conspicuous act of gallantry, Havildar Jesudasan was awarded the Vir Chakra.

The 1965 war also marked the introduction of the Bofors 40mm L/70 gun into Indian service. This upgraded version of the venerable 40mm Bofors gun offered improved performance and would become a mainstay of India's AD inventory for many years to come. Its acquisition in 1965 was a timely enhancement to the AD firepower.

Regimental actions also tell a story of effectiveness. The 26 Air Defence Regiment, which had seen service in 1962, was deployed in the Eastern theatre during the 1965 war. Its units engaged six PAF F-86 Sabres and were credited with shooting down two of them. The 27 Air Defence Regiment (which had been renamed from the 3rd Indian LAA Regiment in February 1965) was deployed in various AD roles in the Western Sector. Its gunners performed with distinction, earning two Vir Chakras, two Sena Medals, and five Mentions in Despatches for their actions during the conflict.

CHAPTER 35

◆◆◆

The Missile Age and Doctrinal Evolution (1971–1993)

The 1971 Indo-Pak War

The 1971 Indo-Pak War stands as a watershed moment in the history of Indian Air Defence. Drawing lessons from previous conflicts and benefiting from a concerted modernisation effort, AD capabilities took a significant leap forward. This war witnessed the widespread deployment of new technologies, including early surface-to-air missile (SAM) systems and advanced radar-guided guns, fundamentally altering the character of air defence operations and contributing significantly to India's decisive victory.

Several key weapon systems were inducted during this era, representing a paradigm shift in AD capabilities:

> **Kvadrat (SA-6 "Gainful") SAM System:** This Soviet-origin mobile SAM system provided medium-range air defence, capable of engaging aircraft at higher altitudes and longer ranges than previously possible with guns alone. Its mobility allowed it to accompany advancing mechanised formations, a crucial capability.
>
> **ZSU-23-4B "Shilka" Self-Propelled Anti-Aircraft Gun (SPAAG)**: Another Soviet system, the Shilka, equipped

with four radar-guided 23mm cannons, offered highly effective, all-weather, mobile defence against low-flying aircraft and helicopters. Its rapid reaction time and high rate of fire made it a formidable asset.

ZU-23-2B Towed Anti-Aircraft Guns: These twin-barrel 23mm guns provided robust, short-range air defence and were simpler to operate and maintain, complementing the more complex systems.

9K33 Osa-AK (SA-8 "Gecko") SAM System: This highly mobile, short-range, all-weather SAM system was designed to engage low-altitude targets, providing point defence for critical assets and manoeuvre forces.

Tigercat Missile System: Deployed around 1972, this British short-range SAM system further augmented India's missile-based AD capabilities.

While these new missile and radar-guided gun systems represented a significant technological upgrade, the Bofors 40mm L/70 guns continued to form the backbone of the AD artillery, especially for point defence and engaging low-level threats. The combination of these systems provided a more layered and versatile AD capability than ever before. This technological leap from a predominantly gun-based defence in 1965 to a mixed missile-gun inventory in 1971 necessitated new operational doctrines, specialised training, and a more sophisticated command and control structure.

Air Superiority and Ground Support

Indian Air Defence played a pivotal role in the 1971 war by effectively protecting the Indian Air Force (IAF) airbases, vital strategic assets, and advancing ground formations from attacks by the Pakistan Air Force (PAF). This robust AD cover was instrumental in allowing the IAF to achieve and maintain air superiority, particularly in the

Eastern theatre, which proved to be a decisive factor in the swift conclusion of the war and the liberation of Bangladesh.

The performance of specific AD units was exemplary. The 27 Air Defence Regiment, equipped with L-70 guns, was awarded the prestigious battle honour "Amritsar Airfield" for its valiant defence of this critical forward airbase against repeated PAF attacks. The regiment's gunners earned three Vir Chakras, one Sena Medal, and two Vishisht Seva Medals for their actions during the conflict, a testament to their courage and effectiveness.

Another unit that distinguished itself was the 129 Air Defence Regiment. Its gunners earned the regiment the formidable sobriquet "The Sabre Killers" for their success in shooting down PAF aircraft. Notable among these achievements were the downing of an F-104 Starfighter over Dwarka on 9 December 1971, an action for which Battery Havildar Major (BHM) Babu Mali was awarded the Vir Chakra, and the destruction of an F-86 Sabre Jet over Okha on 5 December 1971, for which Naik Dhondiram Bansode also received the Vir Chakra. In total, the regiment was awarded two Vir Chakras during the 1971 war. These individual and unit-level successes highlight the tangible impact of AD on the air war.

(Courtesy: ADGPI)

Anecdote – The "Sparrow" Missions

The 1971 war also witnessed remarkable ingenuity in air operations, exemplified by the "Sparrow" missions conducted by the IAF. These missions involved IAF MiG-21FL aircraft (and possibly some Su-7s) flying at high altitudes to act as airborne radio relays for Canberra bomber formations conducting deep penetration night raids against targets in West Pakistan.

The challenge was that the Canberra bombers, after their bombing runs, would return at very low altitudes to evade Pakistani radar and interceptors. At these low altitudes, and often low on fuel, they were frequently out of direct radio range with their home bases or Air Traffic Control (ATC) in India. This made navigation and recovery extremely hazardous, especially at night and under blackout conditions.

The "Sparrow" MiG-21s, orbiting safely at high altitude within Indian radar cover, bridged this communication gap. They relayed messages between the returning bombers and Indian ground control, providing vital homing instructions, diversions to alternate airfields if necessary, and general situational awareness updates. These missions were crucial for the safe recovery of the strike aircraft and their crews.

An interesting consequence of these operations was the PAF's interpretation of the intercepted high-altitude radio relay communications. Lacking a clear explanation for these signals, and perhaps influenced by the effectiveness of the Indian night bombing campaign, the PAF concluded that the IAF was being assisted by Soviet-loaned Tupolev Tu-126 "Moss" Airborne Warning and Control System (AWACS) aircraft. This belief, though incorrect, persisted for some time and even found its way into some Western aviation analyses. The "Sparrow" missions thus not only showcased IAF's operational innovation but also had an unintended psychological impact on the adversary, demonstrating the value of effective, if unconventional, command, control, and communications in air warfare.

The Indigenous Spark: DRDO's Initial Steps in Radar and Missile Development

The successes of the 1971 war, where newly inducted (though imported) missile systems played a key role, likely provided further impetus to India's nascent indigenous defence research and development efforts. The desire for self-reliance in critical defence technologies was growing, leading to the formal launch of the Integrated Guided Missile Development Programme (IGMDP) in 1982–83, under the visionary leadership of Dr. A.P.J. Abdul Kalam. This ambitious program aimed to develop a range of missile systems, including those with direct applications for air defence.

Among the earliest SAM projects under the IGMDP was the Trishul. Development of this quick-reaction, Short-Range Surface-to-Air Missile commenced in 1983, with the intention of eventually replacing aging Soviet-era systems like the OSA-AK in service with the army and air force. The Trishul project, however, encountered significant technological hurdles. Making the missile effectively skim just five metres above sea waves at supersonic speed for its naval variant proved to be a major challenge. Ensuring consistent tracking radar performance was another persistent issue, with intermittent beam breaks leading to the missile missing its target. Although the Trishul underwent numerous tests, with some 80 flight tests completed by October 2006, and demonstrated certain capabilities, it ultimately did not meet the evolving General Staff Qualitative Requirements (GSQRs) of the Armed Forces. In 2003, the government de-linked it from user service requirements, and it continued as a technology demonstrator project, officially closing in 2008.

Despite not being inducted into operational service, the Trishul project was far from a failure in the broader context of India's technological journey. The project provided invaluable experience, honed critical skills in missile design and development, and generated a wealth of technological knowledge within the Defence Research and Development Organisation (DRDO) and its partner institutions. This hard-won experience and the proven sub-systems from Trishul directly contributed to the success of later, more advanced indigenous SAM programs, such as the Quick Reaction SAM (QRSAM) and the Vertical Launch Short Range SAM (VL-SRSAM).

Another key AD-related missile system conceived under the IGMDP was the Akash medium-range SAM. Its development, initiated in this period, laid the foundation for what would eventually become a mainstay of India's air defence shield in the 21st century.

◆◆◆

Parallel to missile development, DRDO, through its Electronics and Radar Development Establishment (ERDE), also began making strides in indigenous radar technology. The Indian Doppler Radar (INDRA) series was a significant early achievement. The INDRA-I, a mobile surveillance radar designed for detecting low-flying targets, was a landmark project for DRDO as it was the first large radar system designed by the organisation and subsequently produced in large numbers for the Armed Forces. It was followed by the INDRA-II, intended for ground-controlled interception of targets. The development of the sophisticated Rajendra multi-function phased array radar, which would become the heart of the Akash SAM system, also commenced during this period, marking a significant step towards advanced radar capabilities. These early indigenous efforts in both missile and radar technology, while facing their share of challenges, were critical in building the technological base for future self-reliance in air defence. This dual strategy of meeting immediate operational needs through imports while simultaneously investing in long-term indigenous R&D characterised India's approach during this era.

The Groundwork for an Independent Air Defence Corps

The increasing technological sophistication of air defence weapon systems—encompassing advanced radars, complex missile guidance systems, and integrated command and control elements—coupled with the highly specialised nature of air defence operations, began to highlight the limitations of keeping AD as a sub-branch of the Regiment of Artillery. The unique demands of air defence warfare, with its emphasis on rapid reaction times, airspace management, and electronic warfare, increasingly pointed towards the need for a dedicated, specialised corps.

A critical institutional step in this direction was the establishment of the Air Defence & Guided Missile (ADGM) School and Centre at Gopalpur Military Station in Odisha. Formally inaugurated on 1 November 1989, this institution marked a significant milestone in the evolution of Indian Air Defence. The ADGM School provided, for the first time, a dedicated, centralised facility for training personnel from all ranks on the newly inducted and increasingly complex air defence systems. This was a departure from the previous arrangement, where AD training was conducted as part of the broader curriculum at the School of Artillery.

Subsequently, the air defence wing at the School of Artillery, Deolali, was moved to the ADGM School at Gopalpur. This consolidation of AD training into a single, specialised institution was a crucial development. It not only facilitated the development of tailored training syllabi and methodologies for missile and gun-missile systems but also began to foster a distinct identity and professional ethos among air defence personnel. The ADGM School became the intellectual and doctrinal hub for air defence in the Indian Army, playing a vital role in absorbing new technologies, developing operational concepts, and disseminating best practices. This institutionalisation of specialised knowledge and the focused development of a dedicated AD cadre laid the essential human resource and doctrinal foundation for the eventual bifurcation of Air Defence from the Regiment of Artillery and the establishment of an independent Corps of Army Air Defence.

CHAPTER 36

◆◆◆

The Corps of Army Air Defence (1994–2024)

A landmark decision that reshaped the landscape of Indian air defence was the formation of an independent Corps. Following a recommendation by the Army Staff in October 1993, the Corps of Air Defence Artillery (later renamed the Corps of Army Air Defence—AAD) was officially established on 10 January 1994, and is celebrated as its Raising Day. This involved the bifurcation of all air defence units and establishments from the Regiment of Artillery, to which they had historically belonged.

This was not merely an administrative reorganisation; it was a strategic imperative. The creation of a separate AAD Corps recognised air defence as a highly specialized, operationally critical, and technologically advanced combat support arm of the Indian Army.

This independent status allowed for a more focused approach to all aspects of air defence: from the formulation of specific doctrines and operational concepts tailored to the unique challenges of countering aerial threats, to the dedicated procurement of advanced AD systems, and the specialised training of personnel. It provided the AAD with the autonomy and institutional framework necessary to evolve in step with the rapidly changing nature of air warfare.

The same day, 10 January 1994, the headquarters of the new corps, the Directorate General of Air Defence Artillery (later DG AAD), came into being, with Lieutenant General P.K. Pahwa appointed as its first Director General. Air Defence wings at various Army command headquarters were subsequently bifurcated from their artillery counterparts. The Air Defence and Guided Missile (ADGM) School at Gopalpur was granted autonomous status, further cementing its role as the premier training institution for the new Corps. The Corps adopted the inspiring motto "आकाशे शत्रुन् जहि" (Akashe Shatrun Jahi), meaning "Shoot the Enemy in the Air," encapsulating its core mission.

The Army Air Defence College, Gopalpur

The Air Defence & Guided Missile School and Centre at Gopalpur, which had been the crucible for specialised AD training since 1989, was formally rechristened as the Army Air Defence College (AADC) in 1998. The AADC stands as the premier training institution for the Corps of Army Air Defence, responsible for imparting technical and operational knowledge to all ranks. Its mandate extends beyond the Army, as it also trains personnel from the Indian Navy, Indian Air Force, Central Armed Police Forces like the CRPF (Central Reserve

Police Force) and CISF (Central Industrial Security Force), and officers from friendly foreign nations, making it a hub of AD expertise.

The college is equipped with a comprehensive suite of state-of-the-art training aids designed to prepare AD warriors for the complexities of modern air warfare. These include various types of simulators, classroom variants (CRVs) of weapon systems, working models of equipment, cut-sections of radars, guns, and missiles, and actual AD systems used by the Corps. The training inventory covers a wide spectrum of equipment, from the ZSU-23-4B "Shilka" and Tunguska M1 gun-missile systems to L/70 and ZU-23mm guns, OSA-AK SAMs, and the indigenously developed Akash and MRSAM (Barak-8) Surface-to-Air Missile systems. Additionally, the AADC boasts advanced facilities such as computer and electronics labs, combat simulator rooms, sand model rooms for tactical exercises, electronic warfare (EW) labs, and mock-ups of the Akashteer command and control system.

A critical asset for practical training is the Gopalpur Seaward Firing Ranges, which extend about 75 kilometres into the sea, allowing for live firing exercises of various AD weapon systems and outdoor tactical drills. This range is equipped with electro-optical tracking and assessment systems for detailed firing analysis and validation of AD systems, using target drones like the DRDO Lakshya. Recognising the evolving threat landscape, the AADC has also been designated as a Centre of Expertise (CoE) on Counter-Unmanned Aerial Systems (C-UAS) and non-communication aspects of Electronic Warfare.

The AADC plays an undeniably pivotal role in shaping the operational readiness, technical proficiency, and doctrinal thinking of the AAD Corps. It is where raw recruits are transformed into skilled air defenders and where experienced personnel are updated on the latest technologies and tactical innovations. However, the path to training excellence is not without its challenges. Observers have noted areas for improvement, such as enhancing the realism of training scenarios, increasing the availability of training missiles and specialised equipment for hands-on practice, and strengthening inter-service joint training drills, particularly with the air force, to ensure seamless operations in a combined environment.

Air Defence in the 1999 Kargil Conflict

The 1999 Kargil Conflict, fought in the high-altitude, treacherous terrain of the Kargil district in Jammu and Kashmir, presented unique challenges for all arms of the Indian military, including Air Defence. While the conflict did not witness large-scale intervention by the Pakistan Air Force (PAF) against Indian ground positions, the potential for such escalation remained a constant concern, necessitating the deployment of AAD assets to protect Indian forces and vital logistic lines.

In this extremely difficult operational environment, Man-Portable Air Defence Systems (MANPADS) played a crucial role. Systems like the Russian-origin Igla, with their portability and ease of deployment, were particularly suited for providing immediate, short-range air defence to troops operating in rugged, inaccessible mountain posts where heavier AD systems could not be easily positioned. The Igla-S, an improved version, further enhanced these VSHORAD (Very Short Range Air Defence) capabilities. An earlier instance of the Igla's effectiveness by the Indian Army was demonstrated in July–August 1992 during *Operation Trishul Shakti*, when an Igla missile was used to shoot down a Pakistani Army helicopter carrying Brigadier Masood Navid Anwari, then Force Commander Northern Areas, and other senior officers near the Bahadur post in Chulung, significantly impacting Pakistani operations in that sector. While specific AD engagements against PAF fixed-wing aircraft in Kargil were limited, the presence of AD systems acted as a deterrent and provided a measure of security to Indian troops and air operations.

The Kargil conflict underscored the imperative for air defence systems that are not only effective but also highly mobile and adaptable to extreme environmental conditions, particularly in mountainous terrain. The vulnerabilities highlighted during this conflict provided further impetus for the modernisation of India's AD capabilities, including the acceleration of the indigenous Indian Ballistic Missile Defence (BMD) Programme, as the threat of missile escalation in future conflicts became more palpable. The 129 Air Defence Regiment, which had distinguished itself in previous wars, earned its third Vir Chakra during the Kargil War, awarded to Major (later Colonel) G.S. Khot for his exemplary service with Army Aviation, conducting casualty evacuation and air maintenance sorties under heavy enemy fire.

DRDO's Successes – Radars and Missile Systems

This period witnessed a significant maturation of India's indigenous defence R&D capabilities, with the Defence Research and Development Organisation (DRDO) delivering a range of sophisticated radar and missile systems that would form the backbone of the AAD Corps' modernisation. This symbiotic growth, where the newly formed AAD Corps provided a clear "user" focus and DRDO delivered increasingly capable indigenous solutions, was crucial in reducing import dependency for certain categories of AD equipment and fostering a national defence-industrial ecosystem.

Radars

DRDO's Electronics and Radar Development Establishment (LRDE) spearheaded the development of several critical radar systems:

> **Rajendra Radar:** A cornerstone of India's indigenous AD capability, the Rajendra is a multi-function Passive Electronically Scanned Array (PESA) radar. It serves as the primary fire control radar for the Akash SAM system. The Rajendra is capable of 3D target detection, multi-target tracking (up to 64 targets simultaneously), and guiding multiple Akash missiles (up to 8 missiles against 4 targets concurrently) under severe electronic warfare conditions. Its development, in collaboration with institutions like

IIT Delhi for phase shifter design, was a significant achievement in complex radar technology.

Rohini Radar: This is a 3D medium-range surveillance radar operating in the S-band. Mounted on a mobile platform, the Rohini provides Track-While-Scan (TWS) capability for airborne targets up to a range of 150 kilometres and features robust Electronic Counter-Counter Measures (ECCM). It plays a vital role in providing early warning and target data to AD weapon systems.

Arudhra Radar (Medium Power Radar – MPR): The Arudhra is an advanced 4D active phased array multi-function radar. It boasts an instrumented range of 400 kilometres (capable of detecting 2m^2 RCS targets at 300 kilometres) and can track a wide variety of aerial targets, from fighter aircraft to slow-moving objects, from an altitude of 100 meters up to 30 kilometres. Its active aperture phased array with digital beamforming provides electronic scanning in both azimuth and elevation.

Other Indigenous Radars: DRDO has also developed a suite of other radars crucial for air defence, including the 3D Tactical Control Radar (3D TCR) for air defence, Low-Level Lightweight Radars like the Bharani (optimised for mountainous terrain), and Weapon Locating Radars (WLR) which, while primarily for counter-battery fire, can also detect airborne artillery projectiles.

Missile Systems

The Integrated Guided Missile Development Programme (IGMDP) began to bear significant fruit in this era, particularly with the Akash system.

Akash Missile System: This indigenously developed medium-range surface-to-air missile system is a flagship product of the IGMDP. The Akash Mk-1 variant has an operational range of 25–30 kilometres and can engage targets at altitudes up to 18–20 kilometres. It employs command guidance with its dedicated Rajendra radar tracking and illuminating targets. The Akash system is highly mobile, designed for quick deployment, and capable of engaging multiple targets simultaneously. It has been inducted in strength by both the Indian Army, which operates several Akash regiments, and the Indian Air Force.

The Akash system has seen continuous improvement. The Akash-1S variant features an indigenous seeker for enhanced accuracy. Akash Prime offers further upgrades. The next major leap is the Akash-NG (Next Generation), currently under development and expected to enter service around 2026. Akash-NG will feature an extended range of 70–80 kilometres, an Active Electronically Scanned Array (AESA) Multi-Function Radar, a dual-pulse solid rocket motor, and canisterised launch for improved mobility and reaction time.

Indian Ballistic Missile Defence (BMD) Programme: Launched formally in 2000 after the Kargil War, this ambitious programme aims to provide India with a multi-layered defence against ballistic missile attacks. It consists of two primary interceptor tiers:

Prithvi Air Defence (PAD)/Pradyumna: This is an exo-atmospheric interceptor designed to engage incoming ballistic missiles at high altitudes (up to 80 kilometres).

Advanced Air Defence (AAD)/Ashwin: This is an endo-atmospheric interceptor designed to engage missiles at lower altitudes (up to 30 kilometres), providing a second layer of defence. The successful development and testing of these BMD components represent a significant stride in India's strategic defence capabilities.

The Legacy of Trishul: As mentioned earlier, though the Trishul SAM project did not result in large-scale induction, it served as a crucial technology demonstrator. The lessons learned and technologies developed during the Trishul program directly benefited subsequent indigenous SAM projects, notably the Quick Reaction SAM (QRSAM) and the Vertical Launch SRSAM (VL-SRSAM), showcasing how R&D efforts, even if not immediately fruitful in terms of deployment, contribute to long-term capability building.

Advanced Imported and Jointly Developed Systems

While indigenous development gained momentum, India also continued to strategically acquire advanced air defence systems from foreign partners and engage in joint development ventures to meet immediate operational requirements and induct cutting-edge technologies. This pragmatic dual approach ensured that the AAD Corps remained equipped to handle evolving threats.

SPYDER (Surface-to-air Python and Derby): Acquired from Israel, the SPYDER is a quick-reaction, low-level SAM system designed to counter a variety of aerial threats including aircraft, helicopters, UAVs, and precision-guided munitions. It utilises two types of missiles: the Python-5, which employs an advanced electro-optical/imaging infrared (IIR) seeker, and the Derby, an active radar homing missile. The system has an engagement range of up to 15 kilometres and has been inducted by both the Indian Air Force and the Indian Army, providing vital mobile air defence cover.

Barak-8 (MRSAM – Medium Range Surface-to-Air Missile): This is a highly capable medium-range SAM system, jointly developed by India's DRDO and Israel

Aerospace Industries (IAI). The Barak-8 is designed to intercept a wide spectrum of airborne threats, including supersonic anti-ship missiles, aircraft, UAVs, and cruise missiles, at ranges exceeding 70–100 kilometres. It features advanced technologies like an active radar seeker, vertical launch capability for 360° coverage, and networking for cooperative engagement. The MRSAM has been inducted by all three service-the Indian Army, Navy (as LRSAM), and air force-significantly bolstering India's area air defence capabilities.

2K22 Tunguska-M1 (SA-19 "Grison"): To provide close-in protection for its mechanised formations against low-flying aircraft, helicopters, and precision weapons, the Indian Army inducted the Russian Tunguska-M1 self-propelled anti-aircraft gun-missile system. The Tunguska-M1 is a formidable integrated system, combining two twin-barrel 30mm automatic cannons (range up to 4 kilometres) with eight 9M311 series Surface-to-Air Missiles (range up to 10 kilometres). Its tracked chassis allows it to keep pace with tanks and infantry combat vehicles, providing organic air defence in a dynamic battlefield environment.

S-125 Pechora (SA-3 "Goa"): A Soviet-era medium-range SAM system, the Pechora has been in Indian service, primarily with the IAF, since the 1970s. Despite its age, the Pechora has undergone several upgrades to maintain its relevance, particularly against low-flying targets, cruise missiles, and increasingly, drones. It is known for its reliability and effectiveness in certain engagement envelopes. The IAF is reported to operate around 25 squadrons of the Pechora system, indicating its continued importance in India's layered air defence network.

Igla-S (SA-24 "Grinch"): An advanced Russian Man-Portable Air Defence System (MANPADS), the Igla-S is an upgrade over older Igla variants previously in service. It significantly enhances the Very Short Range Air Defence (VSHORAD) capabilities of the Indian Army, particularly for troops operating in high-altitude mountainous terrain along the borders. MANPADS like the Igla provide infantry units and special forces with an organic, immediate-reaction capability against low-flying aerial threats.

Network-Centric Warfare, Joint Ops, and Integration

The post-1990s period, and particularly the aftermath of the 1999 Kargil War, saw a significant evolution in Indian military doctrinal thinking. There was a discernible shift away from older, attritional concepts of warfare towards more dynamic, technology-enabled strategies, influenced by global military trends and India's own operational experiences. This had profound implications for air defence.

Network-Centric Warfare (NCW): Recognising the transformative potential of information technology, the Indian Armed Forces began to embrace the principles of Network-Centric Warfare. The IAF took a lead in this by establishing the Air Force Network (AFNET) in 2010. AFNET is a secure, dedicated digital information grid that replaced older communication systems, forming the backbone for network-centric operations. Riding on AFNET is the Integrated Air Command and Control System (IACCS), a sophisticated automated system for Air Defence operations. IACCS integrates data from a multitude of sources – ground-based radars (military and civilian), airborne sensors (like AWACS/AEW&C aircraft), AD weapon systems, and command and control

(C2) nodes – to create a comprehensive, real-time, unified air situation picture. This shared awareness is crucial for rapid decision-making and effective engagement of aerial threats.

Project Akashteer for the Army: Complementing the IAF's IACCS, the Indian Army embarked on Project Akashteer, an indigenous Air Defence Control & Reporting System developed by Bharat Electronics Limited (BEL). Akashteer is designed to automate the Army's AD control and reporting processes at the tactical level. It integrates the Army's own AD sensors (such as surveillance radars and Akash weapon system radars) and weapon systems into a cohesive tactical C2 network, enhancing situational awareness and engagement efficiency for Army AD units.

Akashteer
(Courtesy: PIB)

Jointness – The Integration of Akashteer and IACCS: A landmark development in India's pursuit of joint military operations is the ongoing integration of the Army's Akashteer system with the IAF's IACCS. This initiative aims to create a truly common air picture accessible at Joint Air Defence Centres (JADC). By fusing data from both army and air force sensors, this integration seeks to eliminate operational seams, reduce the risk of fratricide, optimise weapon employment, and ensure a more robust and resilient national air defence. It is envisaged that the IAF, with its strategic assets and wider surveillance capabilities, will likely take the lead in managing the overall integrated AD battle. Joint exercises, such as Exercise Devil Strike, have been conducted to validate these integrated AD operations and refine joint procedures. This move towards integrated command and control is a direct response to the demands of modern warfare, where the speed, complexity, and lethality of aerial threats necessitate a unified, network-enabled response.

Tactical Data Links (TDLs): Secure and jam-resistant communication is the lifeblood of network-centric operations. Efforts have been made to develop and deploy advanced TDLs. The IAF, for instance, has been working on the indigenous "Vayu Link" system, which utilises India's own Regional Navigation Satellite System (IRNSS), also known as NAVIC, for secure data and voice communication between aircraft and ground stations. This system is designed to enhance situational awareness, enable better coordination during air operations, and crucially, help prevent fratricide (accidental engagement of friendly aircraft). The induction of Software Defined Radios (SDRs) across platforms is another step towards enhancing communication interoperability and security.

The drive towards network-centricity and jointness is not merely about acquiring new technology; it represents a fundamental shift in how air defence is conceptualised and executed. It moves away from standalone weapon systems operating in silos towards an integrated "system of systems," where information superiority and collaborative engagement are key to achieving air dominance and effective defence in a contested airspace. This doctrinal evolution, underpinned by technological advancements, has set the stage for the capabilities demonstrated by Indian air defence in the 21st century.

CHAPTER 37

◆◆◆

Operation Sindoor and Future Frontiers

Operation Sindoor, launched by the Indian Armed Forces on the night of 6–7 May 2025, marked a significant point in India's response to persistent cross-border terrorism. The operation involved precision strikes against nine identified terrorist training camps and infrastructure sites located in Pakistan and Pakistan-occupied Kashmir (PoK). This action was a direct retaliation for a major terrorist attack in Pahalgam, Jammu and Kashmir, on 22 April 2025, which resulted in the tragic loss of 26 civilian lives.

India's offensive component of *Operation Sindoor* utilised advanced stand-off precision weapons. Reports indicate the employment of air-launched cruise missiles such as the SCALP (also known as Storm Shadow) and HAMMER (Highly Agile Modular Munition Extended Range) missiles, likely launched from IAF Rafale fighter jets operating from within Indian airspace. Additionally, SkyStriker loitering munitions were reportedly used to engage specific targets. The selection of these weapons underscored an intent to achieve precision effects while minimising collateral damage and avoiding direct engagement with Pakistani military installations, at least in the initial phase.

Pakistan's response was swift and escalatory, leading to a period of intense aerial exchanges. Starting on 7 May and continuing over subsequent days, Pakistan launched a series of missile and drone attacks targeting Indian military installations and civilian areas across a wide frontage, stretching from Jammu and Kashmir through Punjab and Rajasthan to Gujarat. This retaliation by Pakistan triggered a full-scale activation of India's multi-layered air defence network, turning the situation into a critical test of its capabilities.

Aerial Onslaught: Pakistani Drone and Missile Threats

The Pakistani counter-offensive involved a diverse array of aerial threats, deployed in a manner seemingly designed to probe and overwhelm Indian defences.

Initial Retaliation (May 7–8): Pakistan initiated unprovoked drone and missile attacks against numerous Indian military targets. These included attempts to strike airbases and military stations in locations such as Avantipura, Srinagar, Jammu, Pathankot, Amritsar, Kapurthala, Jalandhar, Ludhiana, Adampur, Bathinda, Chandigarh, Nal (Rajasthan), Phalodi, Uttarlai, and Bhuj.

Escalation with Mass Drone Intrusions (Night of May 8–9): The situation intensified significantly on the intervening night of May 8–9. The Pakistani military conducted multiple airspace violations along the entire western border, accompanied by heavy-calibre weapon fire along the Line of Control (LoC). A particularly notable aspect of this phase was an attempted mass intrusion by an estimated 300–400 Pakistani drones. These drones, reportedly including Turkish-origin systems like the ASISGUARD SONGAR or the Bayraktar TB2/Byker YIHA III kamikaze drones, targeted approximately 36 locations, spanning from Leh in the north to Sir Creek in the south. An armed Pakistani UAV also attempted to target the Bathinda military station, an attack that was neutralised by Indian defences. Simultaneously, Pakistani artillery shelling and armed drone usage continued across various sectors in J&K, causing some Indian Army casualties and injuries.

Further Aggression (Night of May 9–10): Pakistan maintained its aggressive posture on the night of May 9–10, employing UCAVs, drones, long-range weapons, loitering munitions, and fighter aircraft to target Indian military infrastructure and civilian areas. Air intrusion and harassment attack attempts were made at over 26 locations from Srinagar to Naliya (Gujarat). These actions reportedly resulted in limited damage to equipment or personnel at IAF stations in Udhampur, Pathankot, Adampur, and Bhuj. Pakistan also targeted medical centres and school premises within Indian airbases at Srinagar, Avantipura, and Udhampur. Civilian areas were also hit, with Pakistani shelling in Rajouri town resulting in the death of an Additional District Development Commissioner, and damage to property and injuries to civilians reported in Ferozepur and Jalandhar.

High-Speed Missile Attacks (May 10): In the early hours of May 10 (around 1.40 AM IST), Pakistan launched high-speed missile attacks attempting to target airbases in Punjab, India.

This sustained and multi-pronged aerial offensive by Pakistan, utilising a mix of missiles, conventional UAVs, and kamikaze drones, presented a complex and severe challenge to India's air defence network.

India's Multi-Layered Air Defence Response

In response to Pakistan's aerial offensive, India activated its comprehensive and multi-layered air defence shield. This involved the coordinated employment of a wide array of systems, from long-range SAMs to upgraded legacy guns and specialised counter-drone technologies.

S-400 Triumf ("Sudarshan Chakra"): This Russian-origin long-range air defence system formed the outer ring of India's defence. It played a crucial role in detecting and neutralising high-altitude Pakistani drones and missiles at extended ranges, reportedly up to 400 kilometres. The S-400 was credited with intercepting multiple missiles, including a notable instance where it successfully engaged eight incoming missiles. Its ability to track a large number of targets simultaneously and engage threats at various altitudes made it a cornerstone of the strategic defence.

Barak-8 (MRSAM): The jointly developed Indo-Israeli MRSAM provided the next layer of defence, engaging medium-range threats that might have evaded or were beyond the immediate engagement envelope of other systems. With a range of 70–100 kilometres, Barak-8 batteries were deployed to protect key installations and were reportedly effective against incoming loitering munitions and cruise missiles. Frontline bases such as Bathinda were actively defended by MRSAM units.

Akash Missile System: India's indigenous Akash SAM system was extensively deployed by both the army and the air force along the western border and the LoC. It proved highly effective in intercepting a significant number of Pakistani drones and low-flying missiles within its 25–40 kilometres engagement range. The Akash system's mobility, quick reaction time, and ability to engage multiple targets, guided by its Rajendra radar, were critical in foiling numerous attacks and preventing damage in several defended zones.

SPYDER System: Operation Sindoor marked the first confirmed combat use of the Israeli SPYDER short-range SAM system by India. Debris from a Python-5 missile, one of the effectors of the SPYDER system, was found in Lsrwal village, Jalandhar, Punjab. This confirmed its deployment and active use in neutralising Pakistani aerial threats, reportedly including heavy kamikaze drones like the Byker YIHA III, at ranges up to 15 kilometres.

L-70 Guns (Upgraded): The venerable Bofors 40mm L-70 guns, significantly upgraded with new radars, electro-optical sensors, and auto-tracking systems, played a vital frontline role in countering low-altitude UAVs and particularly, drone swarms. Their high rate of fire (240-330 rounds per minute) and the ability to saturate an area with predictive fire proved highly effective against these challenging targets. Reports suggest that L-70s, in conjunction with Shilka systems, were responsible for neutralising over 50 Pakistani drones.

ZU-23-2B Guns & ZSU-23-4 Shilka (Upgraded): These Soviet-era gun systems, the towed ZU-23-2B twin-barrel 23mm guns and the self-propelled ZSU-23-4 Shilka quad-barrel 23mm radar-guided systems, also demonstrated their continued relevance. Upgraded with modern fire control systems, thermal imaging sights, and new proximity-fused ammunition, they were highly effective in countering drone incursions and other low-flying threats. The Shilka's formidable rate of fire (up to 4,000 rounds per minute) with enhanced ammunition made it a potent part of the close-in defence layer.

S-125 Pechora: This time-tested Soviet-era SAM system, operated by the IAF and upgraded over the years, was also deployed during the escalation. Its effectiveness against low- to medium-altitude targets, including drones, and its proven reliability and rapid deployment capability, made it a valuable asset in establishing a defensive perimeter.

DRDO Anti-Drone Systems/Counter-UAS (C-UAS) Grid: Beyond traditional guns and missiles, India deployed specialised C-UAS equipment, forming an Integrated Counter-UAS Grid. This included advanced radar and electro-optical sensors for drone detection and tracking, as well as non-kinetic means such as jammers (to disrupt command and control or navigation signals like GPS) and potentially spoofers. Man-Portable Counter-Drone Systems (MPCDS), inducted in 2024, which can jam and disable hostile UAVs, also contributed to this layered defence. While specific use of Directed Energy Weapons (DEWs) during *Operation Sindoor* is not explicitly confirmed in available materials, India has been developing such capabilities,

The overall assessment from available reports indicates a high degree of success for the Indian air defence network. Phrases like "every single missile was neutralised" and reports of over 500 hostile drones and multiple missile strikes being intercepted suggest that the multi-layered system performed effectively, preventing widespread damage to critical infrastructure and military assets. This performance was not just about individual system capabilities but, crucially, about their integrated and networked operation.

The Synergy of IACCS, Akashteer, and the Integrated Counter-UAS Grid

Operation Sindoor is a powerful demonstration of India's maturing network-centric air defence capabilities. The successful repulsion of a large-scale, multi-pronged, and technologically diverse aerial assault was not merely the sum of individual weapon system performances but a testament to their synergistic operation under a unified command and control architecture.

The Indian Air Force's Integrated Air Command and Control System (IACCS) and the Indian Army's Project Akashteer system, along with the overarching Integrated Counter-UAS Grid, were central to this networked defence. These systems facilitate the fusion of data from a multitude of sensors—ground-based radars (both military and civilian), airborne platforms (like AEW&C), and specialised drone detection systems—into a common operational picture. This shared situational awareness, disseminated across services and different AD echelons via high-speed data links and networks like AFNET, enables real-time threat assessment, rapid decision-making, and the coordinated engagement of threats by the most appropriate weapon system. This "defence in depth" philosophy ensures that threats are engaged at multiple stages, increasing the overall probability of kill. The ability to seamlessly integrate information and coordinate responses between the IAF and Army AD assets, a long-term goal, appeared to have reached a new level of operationalisation during this crisis.

This level of integration, moving beyond the deployment of standalone systems to a true "system-of-systems" approach, represents a significant evolution from past conflicts. The sensor-to-shooter cycle is drastically shortened, and weapon systems are employed with greater efficiency and effectiveness.

From the Frontlines

The intensity and nature of the air defence battle during *Operation Sindoor* are further illuminated by specific incidents and observations:

> The discovery of debris from a Python-5 missile seeker head in Jalandhar, Punjab, provided tangible physical evidence of the SPYDER SAM system's active engagement against Pakistani aerial threats, likely heavy drones.
>
> Widely circulated footage reportedly showed Indian Army Air Defence units successfully intercepting and destroying Pakistani Byker YIHA III Kamikaze drones

mid-air near Amritsar, showcasing the effectiveness of close-in weapon systems.

Numerous reports credited the upgraded L-70 and Shilka gun systems with successfully bringing down a large number of Pakistani drones along the Line of Control and the International Border, highlighting the continued utility of modernised legacy systems against specific types of threats.

A crucial aspect of India's strategy during *Operation Sindoor* was not just defensive but also involved proactive measures to degrade Pakistan's AD capabilities. India reportedly employed its own IAI Harop loitering munitions (now also being produced in India) and potentially other systems like the Nagastra to target and neutralise Pakistani air defence radars and systems in locations like Lahore and Karachi. A significant achievement reported was the destruction of a Chinese-supplied HQ-9 long-range air defence system deployed by Pakistan in the Lahore area. This offensive dimension of air defence, often termed Suppression/Destruction of Enemy Air Defences (SEAD/DEAD), demonstrates a mature understanding that robust air defence includes degrading the adversary's ability to project air power or defend its own assets, thereby ensuring greater freedom of action for one's own forces.

Validating Capabilities and Charting the Path Forward

Operation Sindoor, in its entirety, served as an invaluable crucible for validating India's contemporary air defence strategy, technologies, and operational concepts. The successful interception of a large volume and variety of aerial threats underscored the effectiveness of the multi-layered approach and the critical importance of network integration between diverse systems and the armed services. It particularly highlighted the successful synergy between advanced imported systems like the S-400 and Barak-8, and increasingly capable indigenous systems like the Akash SAM and modernised gun systems.

The operation brought into sharp focus the pervasive and evolving threat posed by Unmanned Aerial Vehicles, especially kamikaze drones and potential swarm attacks. This experience will undoubtedly reinforce the ongoing efforts to develop and deploy even more robust, adaptable, and cost-effective counter-UAS solutions. This includes not only kinetic means (guns and missiles) but also a greater emphasis on non-kinetic measures such as advanced electronic warfare suites, jammers, spoofers, and the development of Directed Energy Weapons (DEWs).

Looking ahead, the Indian Army Air Defence is poised for further capability enhancement. The induction of the Akash-NG (Next Generation) SAM system, expected by 2026, with its extended range (70–80 kilometres), AESA radar, and canisterized launchers, will significantly boost medium-to-long range engagement capabilities. Another ambitious indigenous program is Project Kusha, a long-range air defence system designed to intercept hostile aircraft, missiles (including potentially stealthy targets and ballistic missiles) at very long ranges, expected to be deployed by 2028–29.

Continued investment in indigenous Research and Development through DRDO and private industry partners will remain critical. Further strengthening network integration, not just within the AAD and IAF but across all three services, will be a key priority to achieve true jointness in air and missile defence. The development and operationalisation of advanced sensor technologies, AI-driven threat assessment and decision support systems, and resilient communication networks will be essential to stay ahead of the evolving threat curve.

The lessons from *Operation Sindoor* will undoubtedly inform and accelerate these future developments, ensuring that India's "Sentinels of the Sky" remain ever-vigilant and capable of meeting the challenges of the 21st-century battlefield. The successful defence during *Operation Sindoor* was not just a tactical victory; it was a strategic validation of nearly three decades of focused development since the formation of the AAD Corps, and indeed, a culmination of a century of learning and adaptation.

The story of *Operation Sindoor* will be remembered not as a war for air superiority, but as the moment India proved that the sky could, in fact, be held.

CHAPTER 38

◆◆◆

The Ever-Vigilant Sentinels

The journey of India's Air Defence systems, from the rudimentary anti-aircraft guns of the British Indian Army hastily deployed against the backdrop of World War II to the sophisticated, multi-layered, and network-centric shield that guarded the nation's skies during *Operation Sindoor*, is a narrative of remarkable transformation.

It is a story punctuated by the crucible of conflict, driven by technological evolution, and shaped by strategic imperatives. Key inflection points—the baptism of fire in WWII, the hard lessons of 1962, the validation of gunners in 1965, the missile-age successes of 1971, the high-altitude challenges of Kargil, the pivotal formation of the dedicated Corps of Army Air Defence in 1994, the steady rise of indigenous R&D, and the recent comprehensive test during *Operation Sindoor*—all mark significant milestones in this century-long evolution. India has moved from a position of near-total import reliance to possessing a formidable indigenous capability in radars, missiles, and command and control systems, complemented by strategically acquired foreign technologies.

Throughout this transformative arc, one constant has remained: the indomitable spirit and professional dedication of the personnel who man these systems. From the raw courage of Havildar Sham Lal and Gunner Balbir Singh facing Japanese bombs in Singapore 1, to Havildar Athanikal Basil Jesudasan skilfully engaging a Sabrejet over Amritsar in 1965–6, and to the anonymous crews who meticulously operated complex, integrated systems to thwart hundreds of aerial threats during *Operation Sin*door in 2025—the human element has always been paramount. While technology provides the tools, it is the training, skill, adaptability, and unwavering commitment of these "Sentinels of the Sky" that translate technological potential into operational success. The Army Air Defence College at Gopalpur and its predecessors have been instrumental in forging these guardians, though the imperative for continuous enhancement of training realism and jointness remains.

In the contemporary geopolitical landscape, characterised by complex and rapidly evolving aerial threats, a robust, adaptive, and integrated air defence capability is not merely desirable but an indispensable component of India's national security architecture. The ability to protect its sovereign airspace, critical infrastructure, economic assets, and civilian population from coercion or attack from the air is fundamental to India's strategic autonomy and its aspirations as a leading power. The lessons gleaned from *Operation Sindoor*—particularly the validation of the multi-layered, networked approach and the critical role of indigenous systems alongside advanced imports—will undoubtedly shape the future trajectory of India's air defence modernisation.

The continued emphasis on self-reliance through DRDO and private industry, coupled with a relentless pursuit of technological superiority, doctrinal innovation, and inter-service synergy, demonstrates India's unwavering commitment to maintaining a credible, resilient, and formidable air defence shield, ensuring its sentinels remain ever-vigilant against the challenges of today and tomorrow.

Theatre Commands and Future Sentinels

India's air defence doctrine has always stood at the intersection of technology and turf. With systems operated across the army, air force, and navy—each with its own protocols, platforms, and operational silos—the architecture has often been more a mosaic than a monolith. But with the Indian defence establishment now moving, in principle, toward the Theatre Command model, that equation is set to change—and Air Defence will likely be one of the most profoundly transformed domains.

Operation Sindoor offered a glimpse of what jointness can look like in practice. Air force interceptors were scrambled in coordination with Army AD units. Naval radar inputs contributed to IACCS feeds. Live threat matrices were shared across platforms, services, and commands. It worked. But it also revealed the limits of inter-service cooperation without formal structural integration. Messages had to be relayed, decisions cross-validated, and asset availability negotiated across vertical chains. It was a win—but not an effortless one.

Enter the Theatre Command doctrine.

The premise is simple: structure India's vast military forces not around service identities, but geographic or functional theatres of operation. Each theatre would combine assets from the army, navy, and air force under a unified command, streamlining decision-making, eliminating redundancy, and enhancing response time.

In the context of Air Defence, this could be revolutionary.

Instead of the army operating short-range quick reaction systems, the navy guarding seaborne corridors, and the air force running the strategic grid, a future Theatre Air Defence Command could unify all radar assets under one fused surveillance picture, all interceptors, SAM batteries, and EW systems under a single operational logic, and all AD decision-making under one commander, regardless of service background.

It would also integrate space-based early warning, cyber support, and Counter-UAS units into a single doctrinal tree, turning air defence from a service support function into a core combat capability with its own theatre-level command presence.

Such a change, however, is not just about wiring. It's about culture.

For decades, each service has developed its own AD philosophy. The Army sees it as close-in protection for mobile formations.

The Air Force sees it as territorial denial and early warning. The Navy sees it as layered defence for fleet movement. Unifying these philosophies will require doctrinal consensus, shared training, and reimagined career paths so that a radar operator in Leh understands his counterpart aboard a naval frigate in the Bay of Bengal as part of the same grid, not another service.

The creation of a Joint Air Defence Command (JADC)—previously proposed but shelved—is now being quietly reconsidered in some quarters. It would likely emerge first as a functional command, overseeing integration of AD assets across existing theatre lines, and later evolve into its own theatre entity with strategic and tactical mandates.

Crucially, this reform must also tie into India's space-based surveillance assets and ballistic missile defence programme. The Air Defence doctrine of the future won't just need to intercept cruise missiles and UAVs—it will need to account for hypersonics, satellite-denial operations, and sub-orbital threats. That requires not just jointness, but true fusion across land, air, sea, cyber, and space.

Of course, questions remain: Who will lead such a command? What will be the balance of power between services? Will civilian oversight structures adapt quickly enough?

But what's certain is this: in a post-*Sindoor* India, where airspace is now understood as a daily domain of contest, the future of air defence can no longer afford service-wise compartmentalisation. It must evolve into a nationwide, theatre-driven, mission-oriented network.

Because in the wars to come, the sky won't wait for inter-service coordination. And neither will the missile.

EPILOGUE I

◆◆◆

The Sky That Holds

> In ancient times, men looked up at the stars to divine fate. Today, they look up hoping someone is watching the sky for them.

Air defence is built for war—but the infrastructure it creates, the vigilance it maintains, and the reach it commands have unexpected relevance even when there's no enemy.

In times of natural disaster—cyclones, tsunamis, earthquakes—the tools of air defence often become silent responders. Radar networks are repurposed in many places, to monitor weather anomalies, wind patterns, and even high-speed debris. In India, air defence command structures have on occasion supported aerial evacuations, relief logistics, and rapid deployment of shelters, particularly during floods and landslides in the Northeast and coastal regions.

The discipline and coordination that define air defence units make them ideal for operating in chaos. The same soldiers trained to calculate missile trajectories are often those helping guide rescue helicopters through turbulent skies. In this way, the shield built for bombs becomes a scaffold for rescue.

◆◆◆

But what about more cosmic threats—asteroids, space debris, rogue satellites? Is there really a role for air defence when the sky falls in a more literal, astronomical sense?

To date, no asteroid has ever been "shot down" by a missile defence system. The scale, speed, and trajectory of such objects make interception from Earth's surface technologically improbable, if not impossible, at least with current systems. But that hasn't stopped us from trying to get ahead of the threat.

In 2022, NASA's DART mission (Double Asteroid Redirection Test) deliberately crashed a spacecraft into an asteroid moonlet (Dimorphos) to see if its course could be altered. It worked. The asteroid's orbit shifted slightly—a proof of concept that planetary defence is no longer science fiction, but a developing capability.

Russia, China, and the U.S. all monitor near-earth objects (NEOs) through dual-use defence satellites. India's own NETRA project, a space situational awareness initiative, is part of a growing effort to track orbital threats—not just enemy assets, but falling satellites and untracked debris that could harm infrastructure or even re-enter Earth's atmosphere.

Could an interceptor missile like a Prithvi or a THAAD shoot down an asteroid? Unlikely. Could we someday deploy space-based kinetic or laser weapons to nudge celestial bodies off course? Possibly. But more realistically, air defence's contribution lies in detection, coordination, early warning, and possibly, in the future, global response protocols.

So while we haven't yet seen a real-life version of *Armageddon* or *Don't Look Up*, the lines between military defence and planetary protection are slowly converging.

Whether it's a drone, a missile, or a chunk of iron hurtling from the Kuiper Belt, the logic is the same: see it early, understand it quickly, act decisively.

The Aliens Are Coming

It sounds far-fetched. And yet, if there's one thing that science fiction has taught us—across cultures, languages, and decades—it's that the arrival of the "other" is rarely announced. And when it comes, the first to know, the first to act, the first to fall or defend—will be the air defence sentinels.

From H.G. Wells' *The War of the Worlds* to Spielberg's *War of the Worlds*, from *Arrival* to *Independence Day*, from *Prometheus* to *Battlestar Galactica*, our speculative imagination has always known this: the first contact is not with diplomats or philosophers. It is with radars. With NORAD. With scrambling interceptors and malfunctioning satellites. With sirens in the night.

And most hauntingly, in Liu Cixin's *The Three-Body Problem* trilogy, the idea of extraterrestrial contact is not hopeful, but devastating. There, humanity doesn't prepare to greet the stars—it prepares to hide from them. The first act of survival is to prevent detection. The second is to prepare defences. Cixin's message is chilling and clear: the universe is not empty—it's dark because it's dangerous.

So what happens when we're seen?

That question, once the domain of fiction, is inching toward reality. We now have deep space listening posts, planetary defence protocols, and space situational awareness programmes. And while they're tuned more to asteroids and debris than alien fleets, the principle is the same: see early, respond fast, adapt endlessly.

◆◆◆

It is not for nothing that the U.S. renamed its Air Force Space Command as Space Force. Or that China, Russia, and India are all building space-integrated air defence systems. Quietly, perhaps even unconsciously, the world is shifting its military gaze upward and outward.

Because if aliens ever do come—not as invaders, necessarily, but as unknowable presences—the first to respond will not be the United Nations. It will be a radar technician at a missile base. A satellite warning node. An autonomous drone tasked with interception. The same systems that track drones over Barmer today may one day scan for something far stranger over the Pacific.

And in that moment, humanity's old reflexes will return. The instinct to shield. The reflex to observe. The agonising question: is this a threat, or a visitor?

Air Defence will be the custodian of that choice.

Not because it's the most powerful arm of state, but because it is the one most accustomed to ambiguity. Air defenders live in grey zones. They decide in seconds. They act on half a signal. They're trained to shoot without fury, and to wait without flinching. They are already the ones who watch the sky without looking away.

In that sense, the future of air defence is not just national. It is species-wide.

Perhaps we will never see alien ships descend. Perhaps they are waiting. Perhaps they are watching. Or perhaps they are already here—in bacteria, in signals, in quantum ripples we haven't learned to read.

But if they come, the question won't be if we can talk to them. It will be:

Did we see them in time?

Were we ready?

And who held the sky when it mattered most?

Because in the end, it may not be gods or soldiers or diplomats who hold the line between us and the unknown.

◆◆◆

It may be the silent watchers, behind radar screens, inside bunkers, on mountaintops and sea decks—those who were trained not to greet the world, but to guard it.

If the aliens are coming, they may arrive in peace.

But if they don't, it is the Air Defence Sentinels who will write the first chapter of that encounter.

And they must be ready—not for conquest, but for contact.

Not for vengeance, but for vigilance.

◆◆◆

Air defence is not just a military function—it is a pact between the state and its people. A promise that someone is watching. That danger will be met not with panic, but with precision. That a shield, though unseen, stands overhead.

This primer began with a simple question: What is air defence? It ends with a simpler truth:

Air defence is the difference between silence and sirens.

Between a sky that threatens—and a sky that holds.

EPILOGUE II

America's Golden Dome

◆◆◆

21 May 2025

The world woke up to a headline that felt both futuristic and familiar: President Donald Trump had selected a design for the United States' most ambitious air defence project to date—an orbital shield called the "Golden Dome." Announced in a White House press conference flanked by Space Force generals and American flags, it wasn't just the unveiling of a new weapons system—it was the political christening of an idea as old as Cold War paranoia and as new as tomorrow's AI: that the skies above could be locked, controlled, and weaponised for absolute security.

The name itself—Golden Dome—was no accident. It echoed Israel's Iron Dome, which has become synonymous with modern missile interception and layered defence. But while the Iron Dome shoots down short-range rockets with ground-based interceptors, the Golden Dome is something else entirely: a space-based air defence architecture, built not to protect a city but an entire continent. Perhaps, in its designers' vision, even the entire Western world.

According to the details emerging from the Oval Office, the Golden Dome will consist of a vast constellation of satellites designed to detect, track, and intercept enemy missiles—particularly hypersonic and intercontinental ballistic missiles (ICBMs)—from space, before they can reach American soil. In essence, it is a resurrection of Ronald Reagan's controversial 1980s Strategic Defense Initiative—better known as "Star Wars"—only this time with better sensors, faster processors, and exponentially more powerful launch platforms.

Trump, in his trademark flair, claimed the shield would "protect our homeland" and "make space wars a reality." Behind the headline-grabbing rhetoric, though, lay a far more complex and consequential doctrine: the militarisation of near-Earth orbit as the next true theatre of deterrence.

The man tapped to lead this vision is General Michael Guetlein, a seasoned officer of the US Space Force, now elevated to oversee one of the most expensive defence projects in American history—at a projected cost of $175 billion. His task? To build and operationalise the Golden Dome by January 2029, the not-so-subtle implied deadline being the end of Trump's second presidential term—should he win re-election.

The Golden Dome is expected to integrate "next-generation technologies"—from satellite-based early warning radars and AI-enhanced target recognition to kinetic interceptors and perhaps even directed-energy weapons that can destroy targets at the speed of light. According to reports, the system may also include orbiting drone relays and swarm-capable interceptors that launch in microseconds to target hostile warheads, drones, or even rival satellites.

But while the technical ambition is staggering, the strategic message is louder: the U.S. intends to dominate space not just economically, but defensively, by turning Earth's orbit into a hard boundary line, one that missiles—and rival intentions—cannot cross without cost.

Predictably, the announcement sent geopolitical ripples across the globe.

Russia and China responded with sharp warnings. The Kremlin declared that such unilateral militarisation could undermine decades of nuclear arms control agreements and spark a renewed arms race in space. Beijing, in even sterner language, said it was "seriously concerned" that the U.S. was transforming its own defence from a shield into a platform for orbital hegemony. Both countries reiterated their commitment to keeping space a "peaceful domain," while simultaneously accelerating their own space weapons programs.

Closer to home, the reactions were split. American defence hawks and military contractors hailed the announcement as "visionary" and "inevitable." Critics called it a dangerously expensive fantasy, warning that it could provoke adversaries more than protect the homeland. Some defence analysts questioned its feasibility—citing the challenge of neutralising hypersonic missiles mid-flight from orbit, the immense cost of launch logistics, and the vulnerability of satellites themselves to cyberwarfare, kinetic strikes, or anti-satellite missiles.

Yet for all the debate, the symbolism of the Golden Dome is undeniable. In an age where war is as much about psychological reassurance as kinetic threat, building a space-based dome offers a clear message: no sky is too high to fortify.

But it also raises haunting questions. What happens when other countries—provoked or inspired—build domes of their own? What treaties will fracture? What new rules will need to be invented, or broken, to govern war in orbit? And who, ultimately, decides where defence ends and domination begins?

For now, the Golden Dome remains a design, a promise, a warning. But in the years to come, as it slowly takes shape in orbit—satellite by satellite, launch by launch—it may well become the most visible weapon not of war, but of how we choose to imagine peace in the twenty-first century.

APPENDIX

◆◆◆

The Indian Shield—A Layered Arsenal

India's air defence structure is layered—designed so that no single failure results in catastrophe. Each layer addresses a different kind of threat at a different distance, from the long reach of ballistic missiles to the near-invisibility of drones and loitering munitions. Here's an overview of the major systems currently in operation or nearing deployment.

Long-Range Air Defence Systems (Above 150 kilometres)

S-400 Triumf (Russia)
Range: Up to 400 kilometres (with 40N6E missile)
Target: Aircraft, cruise missiles, ballistic missiles
Status: Inducted; five regiments ordered
Notes: Capable of engaging multiple targets simultaneously across altitudes and sectors; forms the backbone of India's outer AD envelope.

Ballistic Missile Defence (BMD) – Phase I (Indigenous)

PAD (Prithvi Air Defence) – Exo-atmospheric interceptor

AAD (Advanced Air Defence) – Endo-atmospheric interceptor
Range: PAD – up to 200 kilometres altitude; AAD – up to 30 kilometres altitude
Status: Tested; awaits operational deployment
Notes: Intended for city-level protection from ballistic missile strikes (e.g., New Delhi, Mumbai); to be developed into a two-layer BMD shield.

Medium-Range Systems (30–120 kilometres)

Akash (Indigenous)
Range: ~30 kilometres
Target: Aircraft, UAVs, cruise missiles
Status: Deployed with the army and the IAF
Notes: All-weather, networked SAM system; capable of protecting large static assets such as airfields and depots.

MR-SAM/Barak 8 (India-Israel)
Range: 70–100 kilometres
Target: Aircraft, cruise missiles, UAVs
Status: Inducted by IAF, army, navy
Notes: Extremely agile; ideal for fleet and base protection; adaptable to mobile platforms.

SPYDER SR/MR (Israel)
Range: 15–50 kilometres
Target: Low-flying targets, drones
Status Operational with the Indian Air Force
Notes: Rapid-reaction system; effective against precision-guided munitions.

Short-Range and Quick Reaction Systems (Up to 25 kilometres)

QRSAM (Indigenous)
Range: ~25–30 kilometres
Target: Aircraft, helicopters, UAVs

Status: Final trials completed; army induction imminent
Notes: High-mobility, road-mobile system for protecting mechanised columns and field formations.

VL-SRSAM (Vertical Launch – Short Range SAM)
Range: ~40 kilometres
Target: Sea-skimming missiles, aircraft
Status: Deployed with the Indian Navy
Notes: Designed to replace the ageing Barak-1; now adapted for land use.

Point Defence and Legacy Systems

ZSU-23-4 Shilka (Soviet origin)
Range: ~2.5 kilometres (gun-based)
Target: Low-flying aircraft and helicopters
Status: Upgraded variant in service
Notes: Radar-guided AA gun system; useful for final-layer base protection.

L-70 Bofors Guns
Range: ~3–4 kilometres
Status: Still in use; being gradually replaced
Notes: Paired with upgraded fire-control radars for better accuracy.

Igla MANPADS (Shoulder-fired, Russian origin)
Range: ~5 kilometres
Status: Used by the army and the air force
Notes: Effective for quick response against helicopters, slow drones

Early Warning and Support Systems

Netra AEW&C (Indigenous)
Platform: Embraer EMB-145
Range: 300–400 kilometres surveillance coverage
Role: Airborne early warning, battle management
Notes: Complements ground radar and improves threat response time.

IACCS (Integrated Air Command and Control System)
Role: Centralised, real-time command integration of all air defence and surveillance systems
Status: Operational across all five operational commands
Notes: Backbone of India's digital air warfare grid.

Upcoming and Strategic Projects

XR-SAM (Extended Range SAM) – Bridging the gap between Akash and S-400 (Range: 250–300 kilometres)

Hypersonic Interceptor Projects – Early-stage, aimed at countering Mach 5+ threats

Indigenous BMD Phase II – Targeting longer-range ballistic threats with satellite tracking support

This arsenal represents not just a collection of systems, but a philosophy: no threat is too small, no response should be siloed, and every layer must speak to the others. The Indian shield is still evolving—but it is now unmistakably strategic, modern, and Indian in character.

Unfolded

◆◆◆

Written for the enthusiast—student, young adult, or any curious reader, regardless of age—the UNFOLDED primers are designed to be engaging, informative, and a stepping stone to further reading on a complex or topical subject.

While the editorial team makes every effort to vet the information in these guides, if the informed reader would like to point out any errors or inconsistencies or share more information, the team welcomes their suggestions at service@thebrowser.org.

About the Author

Co-author of *The POW Who Saved Kashmir—Unsung Saga of Sher Bacha Brig Pritam Singh, MC*, and a software engineer-turned-entrepreneur working in India's "Book Industry" for the last three decades, Pankaj and his wife Deep together run The Browser, an indie publishing house and bookstore based in Chandigarh.

Having ventured into publishing in 2018, initially with a focus on military publishing through their Fauji Days (*faujidays.com*) platform, and then into publishing Classics with their Cuppa Classics imprint (*cuppaclassics.com*) and other fiction, non-fiction and children titles under The Browser imprint (*thebrowser.org*), he believes every book finds its readers once honest effort has been invested in its making.

An avid reader, when not engaged in the world of books and writing, programming in Python keeps his creative juices flowing.

About Fauji Days

◆◆◆

The dearth of good military literature for young Indians—students, cadets, and fauji buffs—is deeply felt.

Many authors, establishments, and publishers must step up to fill this void, and Fauji Days would like to do its utmost, too. A desire to chronicle and celebrate India's military heritage, history, and culture was the genesis of the Fauji Days project in December 2022 by the young digital startup 99beagles, with a focus on publishing books, launching the *faujidays.com* portal, and recording oral history by having youngsters engage our veterans in free-flowing conversations (available on YouTube at @faujidays).

The goal could not be simpler—make good military literature more widespread, accessible, and desirable—but the task could not be tougher. Whether we have succeeded or not is for you to judge, and nothing would make us happier than to hear from you at hq@faujidays.com.

I must thank the entire creative team at 99beagles who have come together to contribute their time and effort to the Fauji Days project—the editors, designers, audio-visual experts, and support crew—without whom the current book you hold would not have seen the light of day.

Even if one young reader draws inspiration from these efforts and is motivated to serve the nation in any capacity, it would be reward enough.

Pankaj P Singh
Chandigarh, May 2025

For more information